Discourses
Volume Six
2019

DISCOURSES:
Writing in the Book of Life
Volume Six: 2019

Yogacharya David R. Hickenbottom

Editor: Ruth M. Lamb, Ph.D

The Cross and The Lotus Publishing
Camano Island, Washington, USA

For permission requests, contact the publisher at:
http://www.crossandlotus.com/contact.html

ISBN: 978-1-957811-07-9 (softcover)
ISBN: 978-1-957811-08-6 (eBook)

All photos courtesy of Carla Hickenbottom Portfolio
unless otherwise attributed (see page 217)

Edited by Ruth Lamb

Book design by Jan Westendorp/Kato Design and Photo (katodesignandphoto.ca)

Cover design by Rob Landers, Ruth Lamb, and Jan Westendorp

Printed and bound in the USA

Published by
The Cross and The Lotus Publishing
Camano Island, Washington, USA
Website: www.crossandlotus.com

Contents

OM TAT SAT AUM

Preface

Yogacharya David, Puri, India, 2013.

We know that each day is a fresh page upon which to write in the Book of Life.

The Divine Mother has descended to earth directly in her form to help devotees ascend to God-realization, and to help the world at large through a difficult transition toward higher spiritual consciousness.

Oh, dearest aspirant, be counted amongst those who rise up to new heights and know the real freedom of Spirit; know a complete renewal of consciousness that has ever been part of your deepest Being.

The nature of living a spiritual life is, in its simplest form, the individual in union with the deepest sense of Self, and then knowing that the same divine Self is present throughout creation. It can range from a gentle nudge of joyful love in the heart to a powerful surge of bliss that makes you escape from the tiny prison of self and expand into God-filled omnipresence.

To break the barrier between human and Divine is the greatest task we have before us.

—YOGACHARYA DAVID

Yogacharya David starts the final months in this body on this planet by sharing joy and his gratitude for the blessings he has received. Yogacharya David speaks of the blessings he received from his guru, Mother Hamilton, and from his second spiritual mother, Swami Satchidananda, and from his param-guru, Paramhansa Yogananda (often called "Master"), and indeed, from other great teachers and masters. How these blessings come seems a mystery. Yogacharya David shares his gratitude and appreciation as we follow his discourses. Yogananda shares a helpful explanation about the blessings of masters:

> Vibrations of other people can be received by an exchange of magnetism. One who comes near a holy person will be benefitted; this is baptism by spiritual magnetism. The saint's thoughts and magnetic aura cast out a vibratory glow that changes the consciousness and brain cells of those who come within range . . . If that attunement is deep enough, even from thousands of miles away, a holy person's uplifting vibrations can be received.[1]

---

1   *The Second Coming of Christ* (p. 107).

Yogacharya David discusses how this latent spiritual awareness can be awakened in us:

> Through my descriptions of Mother and Swamiji, latent spiritual awareness can be awakened in you. Not because you have recently had such an experience, but because a great spiritual potential is sleeping in you and is awakened by such descriptions. You need not have any semblance of that experience, yet somehow you know the truth of it because it awakens the sleeping giant of your God-self and puts you in touch with previously unknown realms. The awakened giant in Mother and Swamiji wakes up the sleeping giant in you!

As we study Yogacharya David's writings, we see a pattern of truth. In his journals, he shares many experiences that affirm Master's words.[2] Here is another vibrant quote from Yogananda:

> The holy Cosmic Vibration, the primal manifestation of transcendental God the Father, emits not only the property of light—the magnificent effulgence of God's divine light and its structural lifetrons and microscopic spiritual eye of supernal consciousness—but also the wonderous sound of Aum, the Word, the great Amen, which is the witness of the Holy Presence . . . Jesus felt his consciousness attuned to the Christ Consciousness to be the "only begotten" reflection of God the Father's Intelligence in the Holy Vibration: he first felt his body as the entire vibratory creation in which his little body was included; then within his cosmic body of all creation, he experienced his

---

2   See *My Spiritual India, Climbing the Sacred Mountain* and *Silence: Entering the Cosmic Sea of Consciousness*.

oneness with God's innate Presence as the Infinite Christ or Universal Intelligence, a magnetic aura of blissful Divine Love in which God's presence holds all beings.[3]

Yogacharya David speaks of his consciousness attuning to the constant Aum that vibrates within his being. He assures us that, "This is the purpose of spiritual masters being in this world—to be transmitting stations for the purifying and uplifting power of Divine Consciousness."[4]

And this Spirit seems to be "calling" Yogacharya David in new ways. He shares: "I have . . . been living more in Spirit, much of the time with just a toehold on the body. God has arranged it this way . . . " and he affirms, 'Of myself, I am nothing; it is my Father who doeth the works' This is a self-evident Truth of which there is no question."

In a series of six volumes of Discourses, Yogacharya David blesses us with his wisdom and his deep understanding of the perilous nature of a climb that can take us to the highest spiritual mountain summits so that we may experience the joy that comes from attunement with Spirit; we too can learn how to reunite soul and spirit; we too can reawaken to who we truly are and reclaim our life-purpose. Let us join Yogacharya David and climb!

Writing in the Book of Life concludes the six-volume series of Discourses, inspired writings shared by Yogacharya David between 2013 and 2019. The volumes are as follows:

- *Discourses—Volume One: 2013–14: Living a Spiritually Rich Life*

- *Discourses—Volume Two: 2015: Re-Union of Soul and Spirit*

---

3   *The Second Coming of Christ* (p. 111).

4   All of Yogacharya David's quotes in the Preface are from these *2019 Discourses.*

- *Discourses—Volume Three: 2016: A True New Birth*

- *Discourses—Volume Four: 2017: Gateway to the Infinite*

- *Discourses—Volume Five: 2018: Standing on the Threshold of Eternity*

- *Discourses—Volume Six: 2019: Writing in the Book of Life*

Regarding the use of images in this publication: Yogacharya David put great care, creativity, time, and intention into selecting images to complement his writings in each and every posting. When preparing his Discourses for publication, we found that certain images from unknown sources, or those which were found to be under copyright, could not be included. Every effort has been made to feature replacement images as close as possible to Yogacharya David's original selections. In a few instances where no similar substitute was available, a picture of Yogacharya David or a beloved saint has been offered instead.[5] Substitute images are designated in the caption by a double asterisk.** For example: Image: Yogacharya David at Anandashram, 2005.** Image attribution is in the References section of the book.

OM TAT SAT AUM

---

5   For more information, see **www.crossandlotus.com**

Introduction

Yogacharya David, Haridwar, India, 2005.

Dear Aspirant,

Whenever you begin a journey, you usually start with a destination in mind, a means of conveyance, and a map or landmarks to indicate that you are on the right path. Those of us following this path have God (Self) Realization as our Goal of goals. Our means of conveyance is God-remembrance, such as chanting God's Name, deepened meditation through Kriya Yoga, universal love and service, loving God, and discernment of Truth.

These writings often come in the early morning: a time when the day is quiet and fresh, an open page upon which to write. These thought-expressions come from an unfathomable Source, welling up from the quiet of the all-pervading Spirit. Reading these words has the power to lead you to the same Source from which they have flowed from within me.

The inspiration that fuels these writings comes to me with great power and clarity; however, mere words are incapable of holding all that is given. It is through inner attunement that the power in the words will lift you into the same Spirit that I experience in Super-consciousness, an uplifting power that is a passageway into realms divine.

Human words and thoughts are imperfect; it is only in pure Spirit that perfection is to be truly found. It is the purpose of these writings that we should rise together in the universal Spirit of God. Come, let us soar together and find truth and beauty unencumbered.

These discourses can act as markers upon your spiritual journey to help make for safe and rapid progress. Unlike a scattered "hunt and peck" approach chosen by many, taking them on "wild goose chases" only to become thoroughly lost, you will receive teachings of the purest quality that speed you on the most direct path to realization. Obstacles often arise, which create challenges for your journey—you can find inspiration here to help you meet those challenges.

These writings contain notes from pilgrimages and journeys that also (reader alert here!) have lessons upon the path embedded in them.[6]

With deepest love and blessings on your journey,
YOGACHARYA DAVID

---

6   This Introduction comes from Yogacharya David's 2013–14 Discourses, Volume One: Living a Spiritually Rich Life.

DISCOURSES

January 3

A FRESH PAGE

Dedication to Swamiji: Yogacharya David and
Swami Satchidananda, Anandashram, 1999.

We know that each day is a fresh page upon which to write in the Book of Life. I think of this coming new year. What does God have in mind for me? One thing I know is making progress on some projects that we have already begun. *My Spiritual India Part II* is coming together as I transcribe my notes from my pilgrimage to India and Anandashram in 1998–9. The first part of *My Spiritual India*, two months of pilgrimage while circumambulating India is already in print. Now, the time I spent at Anandashram with Swami Satchidananda and the wonderful devotees there will be available this coming year—dedicated to Swamiji in celebration of what will be his 100th birthday.

Thanks to Carla and our "Virtual Cross and Lotus Office Staff," Mother Hamilton's talks are being transcribed and readied for publication. There are seven books planned based on her talks and teachings. These have been in the works for some years now and have required time, effort, and expense—they are finally getting ready for print, though there is much yet to do. This will be a tremendous fulfillment for me in response to God and Gurus' command.

There are other writings to digitize. I plan on a series of short topical videos for leading a spiritual life that will be put up on the website. There are videos of Swamiji and interviews of ashram inmates[7] that we plan to make available along with subtitles. We have also been working on updating The Cross and The Lotus website.[8] These are just some of the works we have in motion, and more are in the wings.

Carla and I will spend more time in the desert in the next few months. We are planning to travel to Anandashram in the month of November to celebrate Swami Satchidananda's life. Others have expressed a desire to come to the ashram at that time. To do so, you should write to Swami Muktananda and seek his permission to come. We are blessed to have a spiritual ashram in which we have been treated with such love and hospitality. Papa, Mataji, and Swamiji's spirit continues to live at the ashram and bless all who enter its gates.

With all of this, the most important part of this Work we do for God and Gurus has to do with the individual progress of every aspirant. I have traveled less to the Centers and have been

---

7   "ashram inmates" is a term used in India for ashram residents.

8   Editors Note: The new www.crossandlotus.com website went active in April of 2023.

living more in Spirit, much of the time with just a toehold on the body. God has arranged it this way, and it has been a time for devotee inner attunement. Daily, I feel the greatness and expansion of God's Spirit. In truth, I know that all who actively attune themselves to God, and to God in this form, will receive of this power and the light of the Infinite.

I also know that "Of myself, I am nothing; it is my Father who doeth the works" (John 8:28 and John 14:10, adapted). This is a Self-evident Truth, of which there is no question. The more we attune to God, the more we know that it is God who thinks, breathes, and acts through us. As Papa would say: "Do not think you will be different on the outside now that you are aware that it is the Supreme Consciousness that dwells in you and does all through you." Nevertheless, this realization makes you truly free, fulfilled, and aware of His divine Presence and Bliss coursing throughout your Being, day and night.

This new year brings the promise of the Second Birth to each one who sincerely applies himself or herself to living according to the highest Light he or she knows.

Oh, dearest aspirant, be counted amongst those who rise up to new heights and know the real freedom of Spirit; know a complete renewal of consciousness that has ever been a part of your deepest Being.

You are continually being blessed—as Master once said, "You have God's blessings, you have Gurus' blessings, all that is required now are your blessings!" You have a brand new page upon which to dedicate your life to loving and knowing God: a rare and precious opportunity.

January 6

Paramhansa Yogananda's Birthday!

Beloved Master Paramahansa Yogananda, 1952.**

What a blessed occasion to be focused on our dear Param-guru, Paramhansa Yogananda. Master was born on January 5, and thus we and the world were blessed. Sometimes in our rush to heap accolades upon such a great soul, there is a tendency, especially with a spiritual master, to discount his humanness. This, even though Master, especially rare for the times in which he was writing, gives many detailed glimpses into the workings of his humanity.

Master writes of petitioning God for a revelation, and his tears flow in anguish as he waits for a divine response. This is not the cool calm of a meditating yogi, but a tremendous depth of feeling for God that many can relate to. Being a bhakta, Master had a powerful emotional life, and in his early days could be subject to moods. Sri Yukteswarji worked on his disciple to help him rise above such moods. To have true self-mastery, the influence of moods must be conquered—only emotions directed toward knowing God are cultivated.

Following a grave disappointment brought about by someone close to Master, he actually thought of returning to India after having been in America for just a few years. He took some time and went to Mexico where he thoroughly enjoyed the people. Master was obviously questioning much of the work he had done here in America; he had entered a time of serious doubt. During this uncertainty, Divine Mother told Master he should stay and continue his work in America. This directive changed not only his life but our lives as well. If Master had left, Mother's life would have been completely different. With Mother Hamilton's life so altered, our lives would be radically changed from how they currently are. It all seemed to hang by a thread. Thankfully, Master kept his mind on God and fully surrendered to Divine Mother's will.

We can imagine that Master was above everything, not affected by what came at him—and there was plenty that did come his way. But, the notion that he was above it all would take away from his tremendous accomplishments. True, God could lift him above the tumult of life, but Divine Will ordains for many spiritual masters to be subject to the vicissitudes of life in order to demonstrate how to move through life's many problems: to be an example for keeping the focus of attention on God throughout it all. Even when the body gives out, when friends betray you, and the world mounts a campaign against you, you can find, even as Master found, the inner strength to go on. It is through such self-mastery that you learn about your own potential. To deny a spiritual master's humanity is to negate some of their greatest lessons for you.

Just the fact that Master was born into a family with siblings, a regimented father, and a compassionate mother began a human play that surrounded Master with love and support, as well as many challenges along the way (just as in all families). His desire for freedom and God made school seem slow and plodding. He disappointed his father by not joining the train business—instead, he founded a school based on ancient yogic principles that also incorporated modern education.

Master left India, a rarity in his day, to come to the West to bring the message of a liberating yoga. Many came to hear his talks, a few stayed to really follow his teachings, and of those, a very few devoted their lives to realizing the great truths Master came to bring, and fewer yet fulfilled the ultimate goal—union with God. Disappointment in those who could not, or would not, follow the teachings was part of the human cost for Master.

He was born into, and lived, a human life, and Master, most notably, attained divine liberation. As such, his birth is truly worthy of celebration. Through his words, music, poetry, and his magnificent example, he continues to teach us about universal yoga—or union with God. Through his ongoing emanation of vibrations, he is actively lifting all attuned souls into higher consciousness so that struggling aspirants may become what they are—one with God.

January 9

SPARK OF JOY

Paramhansa Yogananda, Los Angeles, 1925.**

Four years ago, I wrote several postings about the joy of tidy-ing—being impressed with Marie Kondo's methods and spirit for sorting and organizing.[9] The results were amazing not only for me but for many others as well. The basic method is to gather everything of a kind—all your clothes for instance—and make a big pile of them. Then, handle each item individually, fine-tuning your awareness of what items bring you a spark of joy. When joy is felt, you keep it—otherwise, you give gratitude for

---

[9]   *The Life-Changing Magic of Tidying Up.*

what it has brought to you and pass it on. That way, you end up being surrounded by only those items that bring you joy.

Recently, Netflix released a series featuring Marie Kondo and the way her methods and her spirit produce results that are not only practical but also change relationships and lives in significant and positive ways.[10] Having experienced the surprising power of "tidying" (a seemingly innocuous word for initiating such amazing results), I have continued to be impressed with Marie and her methods. I am still working on getting it right in my office, to have only those things that give me joy and to have a place for everything—I have too much paper. I have made a renewed purpose of being tidy in all parts of the house, including my office, and some work in the garage as well—I am still a work of tidying in progress.

The idea of choosing only those things that give you joy with your possessions is wonderful. Then the idea came, why not choose joy in all categories of life? Using the same principles and being mindful of what brings you joy in relationships, work, spending money, recreation, and your spiritual life—taking each, one by one, and feeling the quality of its "fabric," how it fits, and then discerning if it brings you real joy versus doing things out of habit, restless energy, or lethargy.

Think back on your life. Consider if you had carefully evaluated each choice you made while being calm and finetuning your intuition for what brings you real joy. How different my life would have been if I had done that! Some people truly have an inborn sense of purity and know what right-action is, right-relationship, right-work, right-food, and what to imbibe. Many others are more mixed in their understanding, gradually learning to pay more attention in all areas of life to what works—what brings joy. Then there are some who seem to have no built-in discernment at all—in fact, their directional compass seems to point south

---

10   *Tidying Up with Marie Kondo.*

instead of north and they consistently make decisions that bring pain and misery.

Many confuse pleasure with joy, but pleasure is temporary and does not bring real joy. Drinking alcohol, using drugs, having easy sex, or binging on food gives immediate gratification but then you look at the after-effects, such as making poor decisions, hangovers, and being under the power of an addiction—those choices definitely do not bring joy. Some get "drunk" with money-desire—wanting or having it—and some with power and control. Others feel an attraction for someone, but it is not the right relationship for you; however, the temptation for pleasure and forbidden fruit is strong.

Say "Yes" to some things and "No" to choices that do not bring joy. The more you work on conscious living and choosing what brings you real joy in life, the more finely tuned your joy-compass becomes. Through practiced intuition, you instantly know when the compass is pointing north to joy. And because you now know that feeling of joy, you have the strength to resist those strong contrary attractions when they try to attach themselves to you, foul your compass, and clutter your life with things that do not bring you joy.

Meditation, exercise, saving money, not watching too much television (Master called it a pest in the home in the early 1950s), and breaking addictions can be difficult in the moment. However, its after-effect is that you feel better, healthier, and more joyful. So, it is really about taking a moment to sense the total package concerning a certain activity. Ask: Does this bring me true joy?

God is ever-new joy and, therefore, is always the right choice. Because God is beyond cause and effect, you can experience this joy-filled freedom independent of circumstances. And due to the fact that God is purity, the more you focus on God, the better your choices are. Some people fear that if they go with God, they give up on having fun in life; their lives will be dull, staid, and constricted. How wrong they are! God, the intelligence that creates this universe, is the power behind all activities, and the pure essence of joy! This choice brings the most exciting and challenging life. When you choose joy, you choose God, and when you choose God, you choose joy. Let us fine-tune our ability to know what brings us that spark of joy in life, and then be its connoisseur.

January 13

EVER-NEW JOY

Master Paramhansa Yogananda
and Rajasi: Joy-Filled Beings, 1938.

The importance of finding joy in life cannot be fully fathomed in a day, a month, or even a lifetime. This is due to the fact that joyful-bliss is part and parcel of God's Being. Since it is an inevitability that we one day discover God within and without, then joy-filled bliss must be in our future. That being the case, and God being all goodness in life, then it only makes sense to accelerate our growth in God as fast as possible!

The nature of living a spiritual life is, in its simplest form, the individual in union with the deepest sense of Self, and then knowing that the same divine Self is present throughout creation. It can range from a gentle nudge of joyful love in the heart to a powerful surge of bliss that makes you escape from the tiny prison of self and expand into God-filled omnipresence.

There are those who do not think they have the time or the interest to know God. But that is only because they have not been properly introduced. To know God is to love Him, and to love Him is to know Him in greater measure. Some have spoken of a Deity that is still a stranger to them; these are "Doctors of Delusion," estranged from their Creator. In reality, they have not done the real work and have no connection with Truth.

Master quoted St. Francis de Sales, "A saint who is sad, is a sad saint." Of course, that does not mean we never suffer grief. Jesus, purveyor of all things God, upon meeting Martha and Mary in their grief over the death of their brother Lazarus, cried in pain, creating what is said to be the shortest sentence in the Bible, "Jesus wept" (John 11:35). Grief, pain, and the heaviness of the world can sometimes be burdens we must carry. However, in finding God as our all and all, then the Divine Presence will be with us in good times and in bad. The more we are focused on our Heavenly Father and Divine Mother, the more we will feel uplifting joy.

Joy does not always need to be expressed through laughter and frivolity; in fact, over-the-top hilarity is many times the opposite of joy—it is a simple release of tension, or an attempt to fit in. A devotee once asked if there were any corrections I would make of her, and I stunned her when I said she laughed too loudly; it did not come across as genuine. Well, a moment before, she had professed that she would do anything to realize God, but it was clear she was not in favor of this observation.

A dear friend from many years ago belonged to a "spirit-filled" church with thousands in attendance each week. She had a bubbly personality and was disturbed when she was driving on the freeway and saw so many unsmiling faces. She would give big smiles and wave at drivers and passengers alike, looking to cheer their days. But, if it is not in your personality to be so gregarious, then you might feel joy in a quiet way. In fact, you may not be able to channel joy through your body as my friend did. Another choice is to let joy draw you deeper within so that you might expand into this powerful experience of joy.

Most importantly, be observant of your own states of consciousness throughout the day. Do you experience a joy-filled Presence in your meditation? With your family and friends? In your work? And all through the day? Or do you limit your joy? Are you a complete stranger to it? Focus on that joyful-bliss that is less contingent on your outer world and streams from your inner world—your connection with God. If joyful-bliss is a stranger to you, make it your business to recover it, for it absolutely exists deep in your Soul as your natural state.

Bliss changes your life in all ways good; joy fills you from the inside out. So, make your environment, your family, your friends, and your life align with God's joy, and He will guide you perfectly in all your ways. Blessings.

January 17

HURRY HARRY: A PARABLE

Pathway through a green forest.**

There was a man named Harry; his nickname was "Hurry Harry." Hurry Harry worked in keeping a large public park. His specific duties included raking a graveled walk and keeping his area looking neat and tidy. As you might imagine from his nickname, Hurry Harry was a nervous, twitchy type of fellow who was easily frustrated by the lack of respect others gave his park. Children kicked rocks; people dropped wrappers and whatnot on the ground. With frustration, he kept his area spit-spot.

Over time, Hurry Harry came to think that his job of repeatedly keeping the park clean did not matter. "Anyone could do this stupid job!" He daydreamed of doing something important in the world, a job others respected and would not trample upon. Now, each piece of trash and disrupted rock on the path he saw as a personal affront. Anger seethed beneath the surface and finally exploded one day when Hurry Harry walked off the job and did not come back.

Of course, with Hurry Harry not there, his part of the park rapidly deteriorated. Other groundskeepers came to the Master Groundskeeper; they wanted to put in extra time to take care of Harry's area until someone new could be found. The Master Groundskeeper was not only a master at keeping the park running smoothly, he was also a master psychologist. He had seen how Harry was building into a volcanic existential crisis but he knew that he must let things play themselves out. So, he took a risky stand and left that part of the park to take care of itself: without Harry or anyone else taking his place.

Hurry Harry cast about in the world for some time. He did not find that he was any more respected at other things he did than he had been at the park. In fact, other situations only seemed worse to him. He thought back on the park—that he really did love—and how beautiful it was, how fortunate he was to work there. He was a part of something noble, facilitating nature's splendor and enabling harried people to find peace and recreation under the trees surrounded by flowering plants. Even the graveled path grew into something of a hallowed memory for Harry.

One day, Harry visited the park with others from the city, fully expecting the duties of his area to have been taken over by another. To his horror, he saw everything topsy-turvy! The rest of the park was splendiferous, as he would expect. But his area was in shambles. Good people avoided his part of the park; hooligans had taken it over in its neglect. Harry furiously stomped his way to the Master Groundskeeper and demanded to know why that beloved part of the park had fallen into such a state of disrepair and disrepute!

The Master Groundskeeper patiently heard Harry out. When Harry had wound down, he simply said, "Why Harry, that is your job. Why blame me?" It dawned upon Harry that his role in the park was essential; it was his neglect that made possible this nightmarish scene. It took time and determination for Harry to bring that part of the park back into order.

Now, instead of calling him Hurry Harry, others used his proper name, Harold. Harold means the ruler of an army, and the army he benevolently ruled was his part of the park. As he courageously brought back order and cleanliness, the hooligans left, and good people found it safe and inviting again. Other groundskeepers were inspired by Harold's calm, clearheaded approach to his work. And while he could occasionally be irritated (but mostly just found it sad) when others disrespected the park, he never again doubted that this was exactly why he was needed. The End. (Well, just the beginning for the renewed Harold!)

January 20

PARABHAKTI: THE LORD IS ONE

Tree of Life: Ascending the spinal tree into
Parabhakti, painting by Tamasin Ramsay.

Someone wrote, apologizing for "momentarily falling for the guise of (my being) a human." But, why should I not be human? It is the mind only that divides up this world and says, "This is human and this other is Divine." Breaking the barrier between human and Divine is the greatest task we have before us.

A dualistic perspective tells us: "The human in me is not Divine, and the Divine I sometimes comprehend is not the human." Our experience tends to bear this out—when you know the human self, you feel that you are only an individual, separate from God. When you are lifted up into God-consciousness, it is something so completely different—better, higher, purer—that you cannot think of the human and Divine as being in the same category.

But can a living branch ever say to the tree, I am not of you? If the branch were to really think on it—its life must come from the trunk, which has its source in the roots; in fact, they are all the same organism. This is to say, every individual soul is rooted in the Divine Essence and can never be separate—or else it would cease to live; it would no longer be.

It is the task of the mind to practice spiritual methods for realizing a fact that is already so. The mind is limited when it looks at the human and sees it as a separate thing. When the aspirant is devotedly focused on God and is consequently lifted up through bhakti (aspiring for God-vision), and comes to experience God—sometimes within, sometimes without—this is a start.

The bhakti yearns for God with everything he or she has and strives to realize the object of this love and adoration. Through the bhakti's repeatedly touching the fabric of God's Being, the mind is further purified, and now the state of God-experience makes the world seem like a dream.

In this uplifted state of jnana, the mind thinks of the world as an illusion that is not God. The jnani says, "Transcendent God alone is real; all else is false." This high state of the jnani is tremendous, but it too is not our final destination—there is more.

We continue our quest for the universal-vision of God. Being immersed in the transcendent God-experience, the mind is further purified, lifted into the state of para-bhakti, the supreme state of Purushottama.[11] The para-bhakti perceives the transcendent state manifesting as the world, the body, and even as the expression of the ego; all are manifestations of a single, unified life. Now, God is seen operating in the highest consciousness and manifesting itself as all in all. In this supreme Reality, everything is known to be God—within, without, and everywhere about. Established in this supreme Reality, the soul fulfills its highest purpose.

Realized beings exist as living manifestations of these great truths. Saints manifest a bhakti's great love for God and inspire that same love and dedication in others. Some saints become mystics of a higher order; they see the world as no longer real; it is not evil, it is not good, it is simply an illusion that stands in the way of perceiving transcendent Spirit, a thing of unreality. Then there is the universally realized Soul who knows that all is God, and God is all—that the branch is a flawless manifestation of the tree, just as the wave is a natural creation of the ocean.

The mistake is made when the branch thinks of itself as separate from the tree, or the wave from the ocean. This creates a false dichotomy that, in reality, can never be. Those on the upward path see the spiritual master and encounter his or her humanness. The aspirant can project onto the master his or her

---

11   Editor's Note: Purushottama described by Sri Aurobindo in *The Essays on the Gita*: "The Supreme is the Purushottama, eternal beyond all manifestation, infinite beyond all limitation by Time and Space or Causality or any of his numberless qualities of features. But this does not mean that in his supreme eternity he is unconnected with all that happens here, cut off from the world and Nature, aloof from all these beings. He is the supreme ineffable Brahman, he is impersonal self, he is all personal existence. Spirit here and life and matter, soul and Nature and the works of Nature are aspects and movements of his infinite and eternal existence. He is the supreme transcendent Spirit, and all comes into manifestation from him and are his forms and his self-powers (pp. 558–9).

own ignorance, seeing the master as a human being only. In truth, the master is working through an individualized humanity to help universalize the vision of those around by being both human and Divine. Mataji, of Anandashram, was disturbed by what she saw in Papa (Swami Ramdas) when he showed preference for some over others. She had not yet realized that God was working through Papa in the way he brought some close and kept others more at a distance. This did not represent ignorance in Papa. It was not that he did not see God in all. It is simply how God was operating in his form for the highest good of all.

In fact, to be able to function in this world, a fully realized master must show distinctions; it is the nature of creation. For a fully realized master, whether one is close or far away, all are God. A master will even orchestrate difficult situations for the disciple, as did Master Paramhansa Yogananda with Mother Hamilton when he created an invisible barrier between them that lasted for three years. By doing so, he was helping to purify Mother and prepare her for the universal vision. And, as Mother said of Papa, he loved me so much, he was willing to hurt me; "Ramdas crucified the ego in order that the Divine might live."[12] This can sound strange,

---

12   *The Mystical Crucifixion* by The Reverend Mother Yogacharya Mildred Hamilton (p. 32). Editors Note: Mother Hamilton has a very specific meaning in this statement. When her guru Paramhansa Yogananda left his body, Mother Hamilton had not yet reached the highest state of God-realization. In answer to her prayers, she met Swami Ramdas, a realized master from Anandashram, India. Mother Hamilton requested his assistance and guidance. Swami Ramdas agreed but not without testing Mother Hamilton's resolve. After Mother spent many months at the ashram, Swami Ramdas agreed to assist her with taking "the final mile." Mother Hamilton says: "I know what it means to die on my own cross, which is my body. I know what it means to descend into hell, or the subconscious, of my own being. I know what it means to suffer for everything that I had done, not only in this lifetime but through incarnations; certain ones of them paraded before me. And I paid the price. I paid a tremendous price. I died on my own cross, which is my body, but I arose again from the dead. And don't think that is just unique with me, because others have had this experience" (p. 66). Read *The Mystical Crucifixion* to be reminded about the great spiritual nature that is latent within us all.

even wrong, to one who has not experienced it. But it is true, even as a surgeon, when slicing you open, is working to cure you.

So, let us love and strive as bhaktis, discriminate as jnanis, and follow in the steps of great spiritual masters in attaining the universal-vision becoming para-bhaktis: free in the ultimate realization as the human and the Divine merge. Then, no matter where we look, or what we do, there is only One, only God. "Hear, O Israel, the Lord our God. The Lord is one" (Mark 12:29).

January 24

MAKING IT YOUR OWN

This morning's desert sunrise, Arizona.

The desert moonlit scape is a beautiful sight: every bush and rock in sharp relief, a long-legged Jackrabbit lopes through the brush, and not far away, coyotes yip. Even though it is Papa's hour, nature's world is wide awake! (3 a.m., I call it Papa's hour because it was his waking time for so many years at Anandashram).

One of the projects I have been immersed in is typing my diary notes from my 1998–9 pilgrimage to Anandashram. Some days I am transcribing what happened on the very same month and day exactly twenty years before. So fully have I been taken back to that world, there are times when looking up, I half expect to see ashram inmates and workers walking by. Perhaps the palm trees here in the Anza-Borrego Desert add to this associative effect. It has been wonderful to go back to that time, especially my time with Swami Satchidananda at Anandashram.

What an effect he has had on me; how he helped me Godward! With undiminished gratitude, I bow at Swamiji's feet. I am sure that, to many, bowing at another's feet would seem an odd thing to do, yet to me it seems the most natural response to one who exudes such a powerful presence of God—so naturally flowing through his being.

This is the purpose of spiritual masters being in this world—to be transmitting stations for the purifying and uplifting power of Divine Consciousness. I have had professors who have stimulated my brain, waking it up to new thoughts and discoveries. Then there are wonderful people I have known who have impressed me with the quality of their being, making me a better person by just being in their presence. Without taking anything away from these remarkable people, they are like burning candles compared to the sun-like presence of Mother Hamilton and Swamiji.

It is always interesting when I sit and let God write through me as I am doing now; this is not what I had thought to write about at all when I started. But I am very happy to go anywhere God takes me because then I am in His Presence, and that is the most important part of any moment throughout the day. And that brings about a most salient point; we are so used to being filled with ourselves, our thoughts, desires, fears, and habits, that we have a difficult time thinking about submitting our wills to any-thing or anyone else. But that is really the point, God is not any-thing or anyone else—He is you and me in the deepest purest sense.

So, one might then ask, how do I distinguish what is God and what is me? And here may be a very unsatisfactory answer, "You know it when you experience it." As with so many experiences (and this spiritual state of being is even more so because it is such a tremendous transformation), you can describe something, and your word-pictures will trigger someone else's thoughts and feelings, but they are limited by their own experience.

I started out describing the night hours here in the desert and if you were here with me, or have had similar experiences yourself, you would be full of close approximations to what I am talking about. But if you have had no such relevant memories of being in the night desert, then you must fill in as best you can, based on whatever experiences seem close. And if you have had a negative association with a night desert, such as a fear of coyotes or rabbits, for instance, then that will definitely color your picture of what I am describing, producing fear instead of sacred mystery.

But here—this is very true with spiritual experience—there is an additional depth to word-power. Through my descriptions of Mother and Swamiji, latent spiritual awareness can be awakened in you. Not because you have recently had such an experience, but because a great spiritual potential is sleeping in you and is awakened by such descriptions. You need not have had any semblance of that experience, yet somehow you know the truth of it because it awakens that sleeping giant of your God-self and puts you in touch with previously unknown realms. The awakened giant in Mother and Swamiji wakes up the sleeping giant in you! Isn't that remarkable?

When I first met Mother, and then later came into Swamiji's presence, I recognized the awakened God-Self in them, and it stirred something deep in me. Meeting Mother and Swamiji came at two very different times in my life, but there were recognizable similarities in what they awakened in me. When I met Mother, I had no reference for how she affected me; my mind took years to begin to intellectually understand who and what she was. By the time I met Swamiji, I'd had many years with Mother, so it was easier in one sense to mentally understand what I heard, saw, and experienced. Yet, even though that was true, it did not take away the mystery of what God is, or how He operates through His chosen instruments. It is in the nature of these encounters that they stretch, challenge, and change the aspirant in ways that are unfathomable at the time—and all for the good!

So, in humble gratitude, I bow at Mother and Swamiji's feet. In my growing awareness, I stand at a distance and appreciate the mountain-like statures of these two great masters. Through their grace, they have also raised me to new heights of God-perception where I can share in their panoramic vistas. Through who they are in God, they have vouchsafed me entry into the Divinity they have so thoroughly made their own. From their great sacrifices and striving, they invite all of us to embrace this God-vision and make it our own.

January 27

WE WERE ALL IN "DIFFERENT SPACES"

Yogacharya David at Anandashram, 1999.**

continue typing my notes from Anandashram, 20 years ago to the day. It has reminded me of my time there and the transformation I experienced. When it came to Mother's Mahasamadhi Day, coming up on the 31st, I had a very interesting thing happen that demonstrates how God works in mysterious ways.[13] Even seemingly negative behavior by others can be an expression of His will. From my journal:

_____

13   Sanskrit for "great merging," mahasamadhi means to voluntarily and consciously leave one's body in agreement with divine will: to be fully conscious in oneness with God at the moment of exiting the body.

Ram's Play of Grace through Rudeness: January 31, 1998

Yesterday, I sat in a very crowded darshan with Swamiji. Gabriel came in and I patted the only space open that happened to be next to me. Someone from the door wanted to pass a note through the crowded room and was looking at Gabriel to do it. This is a highly unusual thing to happen, but Gabriel, being a pure soul, immediately got up and made his way forward with the note to Swamiji. It is to be noted that Gabriel has pain in his legs which makes sitting down on the floor and rising difficult.

An American devotee came in and headed for Gabriel's spot. I signaled and said, "Gabriel is sitting here." He responded, "Well, I am now!" and sat himself down. At first, I had a flush of anger, then came a resignation to God's will. When Gabriel returned, I got up and signaled that he should take my place on the floor. I reasoned that these visitors had few opportunities, as I have had, for the darshan of this great saint—it felt good to give him my seat.

There was literally no space left in the darshan room, so I left. When I returned to my room, I discovered a half-written fax to be sent for Mother's Mahasamadhi. The fax needed to be completed and taken to town for it to arrive in time for the Seattle Group. Somehow, the fax had slipped out of my mind and I thanked God for enacting the play at Swamiji's darshan so I could complete this important project for Mother.

No Explanation Is Necessary, But Here It Is

Today, the friend who took Gabriel's space came by. He said, "I don't suppose an explanation is necessary about yesterday, but here it is." An odd way to start, I thought. "When I walked in for darshan, I was in one 'space.' You said the spot was for Gabriel and you were in another 'space.' I wasn't thinking very quick, just intent on getting a place to sit; that was the 'space' I was in. Gabriel, up with Swamiji was in another 'space.' Anyway, that is how it all happened; we were all just in different 'spaces.'" I think this was his way of apologizing! I assured him that it all worked out for good. This friendly response emboldened him to say that some shakti must have been working through him. Satisfied now with his own explanation, he shifted to other topics.

I knew he would have to say something to me about the darshan seating incident, but this was such an interesting explanation. I could not have anticipated what he had said in a million years! On a human level, I could have made any number of observations about his "explanation," but in the end—he was right. This was God's shakti power working through him in the situation to maneuver me into completing my writing for Mother and still have time to take it into town and send it out to devotees. Jai Guru!

This play of God's is a fun reminder that no matter the appearance of a thing, God is at work. Sometimes, we are in on the plan, sometimes it is simply knowing there is a plan and that it is all being worked out according to Divine Will. All is in His Keeping. All is in His will. May He lift us into the awareness that His all-loving, all-knowing Presence is with us, no matter what 'space' we may be in or what mask He may wear.

January 31

MOTHER HAMILTON'S 28TH MAHASAMADHI ANNIVERSARY

Easter Group at Bonnie's, Mother Hamilton (center)
behind the children, Seattle, 1977.

Lost in the Common Life of All Which Lives

There are so many things I love about what Mother Hamilton brings to the path of realization. A big part of her focus is the practical approach she practiced and taught. You do not have to move to Kathmandu, shave your head, sell incense on the street corner, or do any of a thousand other questionable things. And while I would have been willing to do any or all of these things if they were necessary to realize God, Mother taught us to practice Kriya Yoga to keep our minds on God and to remain in the world—living lives much as most people do.

A quote I read many years ago from the Bhagavad Gita made a lasting impression on me:

> Whoso is fixed in holiness, self-ruled, pure-hearted, lord of senses and of self, lost in the common life of all which lives—a "Yogayukt"—he is a Saint who wends straight-way to Brahm. Such a one is not touched by taint of deeds. "Nought of myself I do!" Thus, will he think—who holds the truth of truths.[14]

The notion, "Lost in the common life of all which lives," living a normal life, yet spiritually freed, perfected, and established in the Truth of truths—I found this to be so inspiring down through the years. I remember Mother inviting me out for lunch to one of her favorite restaurants, *The Legend Room*. It was a nice restaurant connected to the *Bon Marche* department store in the Northgate Mall, Seattle. The wait staff was very pleasant with Mother, and each time her nearly-full cup of coffee became cool, they brought her a fresh cup (Mother always liked her drinks either very hot or cold; nothing tepid).

We would then walk up through the department store and clerks would say, "Hello Mrs. Hamilton." Mother said she once wondered how clerks remembered her name, then she realized it was because she used a credit card to make purchases and her name was on the card. So much has changed in the world since then. At that time, it was rarer to use a credit card. Mother was also the first person I knew who had a home answering machine. She was, well—modern.

Now, those clerks may have thought that Mother was anything from a good customer to being someone truly special. There were no big signs above Mother that said she was an incarnation

---

14   *The Song Celestial*; or *Bhagavad Gita*. Chapter 5.

of the Divine Mother. In fact, Mother enjoyed meeting people and getting to know them on their own terms. She also enjoyed having her privacy; she did not need or want to be kowtowed to—Mother was *lost in the common life of all which lives.*

When Lahiri Mahasaya first met Babaji, the master said Lahiri Baba needed purification and immediately got to work. Lahiri Mahasaya commented, "Babaji's practical wisdom, I reflected with a quick, reminiscent smile, was ever to the fore."[15] We could easily imagine Babaji walking a few feet above the ground, haloed in light, and never quite human. It is interesting to think that on meeting Babaji, we would be impressed by his practicality. I know with Mother, I was always struck by the firmness of her step, not a few feet off the ground, but solidly treading to her next destination.

Mother once told me that she had made a mistake in her checkbook; fortunately, the error was in her favor, so she was all right (she was not going to be bouncing future checks). I think what is important about these observations is that, while Mother was the most spiritually powerful person I have met: she attained the rare Sahaja Samadhi (the highest realization of God), she raised the dead, healed the sick, and had the capacity to lift devotees into God-consciousness, she also lived a human life, and enjoyed it.

We can all relate to shopping, enjoying a good restaurant, and making a checkbook error. These are everyday events that to Mother were all part of knowing that the world is God; nevertheless, she experienced the world in common ways we all can connect with. This does not lower Mother to be a simple, worldly person; rather, it lifts us up to her view, her realization of the Divinity of life, all of life.

Mother worked outside the home; she was the first woman manager for the telephone company; she married, raised three children—and had surrogate children—friends of her children

---

15   *Autobiography of a Yogi* (p. 196).

who came to the house and were so comfortable, they called her "Mother." Mother had concerns about money, and a challenging relationship with her father, the kind of things that we all interact with on an everyday basis. Mother not only stressed being practical in this world, she openly proclaimed her humanity as well as her divinity.

As Mother said:

> When man knows the truth, he indeed shall be free. And the truth is that you and your Father are one, now. You always were, you are, and you always will be. How can you doubt it? When there is none but He everywhere; it is He, it is He. Open your heart now. This is the highest truth that can be taught to you—to do good, to see good, to purify yourselves in God. All of us fall flat on our face every now and then. I read you a few of my own falls the other night. I thought afterward (you know, the human part of me), *I shouldn't have read all that; it might create a bad impression.* And I thought, well, it's a good example, you see, on the way of man, or rather, of man on his way to the Infinite, because there isn't anybody who doesn't think a wrong thought or make a mistake in the whole universe. And the greatest saint, the greatest Christ, the greatest anything that ever lived, was born in a human body and, therefore, they made mistakes before they became one with the Divine within themselves. It is true. . . . But as long as you keep your love for God and you pick yourself up and you keep on trying, you can make it. And you know that's true because you have, many of you, watched me do it. You have seen it in operation. And if I can do it, being the smallest one in the world, then there isn't one of you here or anywhere that cannot do it. You can become pure, you can become

holy, beautiful, wonderful, filled with joy and laughter. But when you're one with Him, you're anything He makes you. And sometimes you cry for yourself because you are weak. Sometimes you laugh, you take joy in yourself, you love. And this is God.[16]

This is what Mother brought to us: practicality, a human perspective, and the total realization of God. Perfect for the modern Westerner, a perfect message for all. On this January 31st, the anniversary of Mother's Mahasamadhi and a celebration of our divine guru's life and mission, let us honor Mother by removing all false barriers between ourselves and God. Let us live the message she came to deliver when she took incarnation, that *life is God, and God is life*—all of life. Discover your divinity, within and without, and be *lost in the common life of all which lives.*

---

16   Mother Hamilton's quotes can be found on **www.crossandlotus.com**. Yogacharya David notes that this quote is from *The Christ Within*, 1970.

February 3

Fulfilling Your Purpose

Glorious fulfillment of Arjuna's Purpose,
artwork by Vasudeo Pandya, 1932.**

Knowing your purpose in life is essential: lose that purpose and you lose not only your direction in life but also hope, and the value of life itself. A tamasic-depression results in a loss of purpose, or, not caring about what you know should be important. On the other hand, a rajasic-dynamic life may have so many aspirations that there is no real sense of what is important, or essential—it is one massive ball of entangled ideas and energy. Sattvic-calm purpose has clarity, and it keeps the soul grounded in practical actions that are tied to life's greater purpose.

As a soul, you come into a lifetime with goals for what you want to learn and achieve. A goal may or may not rise to the elevation of purpose—purpose speaks to the reason for taking an incarnation. But purpose comes with a burden; if you do not accomplish your purpose in life, it is a terrible letdown to the deepest part of who you are. Buying the latest phone may be a goal but it does not speak to your purpose. Completing a degree, establishing a business, raising children, moving the world forward in some great endeavor, or attaining a high state of realization may be the kinds of things that speak to your purpose—for why you were born.

Purpose is not something that can be handed to you, it is something you must discover for yourself. My Grandfather started a fruit, produce, and trucking business. My father always saw himself going into business with his father, which he did return to when he was discharged from the Coast Guard. My mother said she had thought I would go into business with my father, along with my eldest brother. Although this would have fulfilled her expectations (my father never voiced his thoughts on the topic), it was clear to me that my direction and future were elsewhere.

In my case, from my late teens onward, the only thing that spoke to me about my purpose was Self-realization; everything else in life only made sense to me under that one umbrella. I was willing to do things in the world, as long as they fit in with realizing God. Knowing God was the first thing in my life to which I fully committed myself. While growing up, I played sports, was a student, a Boy Scout, and I worked many hours for my father's business. I played and caroused but nothing I did was wholehearted. I take no pride in that fact. I think I did not get the greatest advantage from any of those activities by not giving it my all. I did not understand it myself. Only when I met Mother did I commit myself to anything fully.

I know that is not everyone's story, and that you have your own way to wend to fulfillment. What is essential is that you know why you have come—as long as you are drawing breath, there is yet purpose for you to fulfill. It is important that you do

not enter the sinkhole of a tamasic mood in which you are unin-
spired. One of my great objections to the drug marijuana is that
it robs the individual of motivation and purpose—complacency
being one of its primary side effects. That fits hand in glove as a
trap for tamasic mood-states, even though it initially brings a kind
of euphoria. To be alive to your purpose brings life-energy, enthu-
siasm, and creativity—all life-affirming attributes.

The other side of that guna-coin is rajasic overstimulation in
which you are busy, busy, busy: with never a minute. In all like-
lihood, if you ask a driven person about purpose, a rajasic person would give a laundry list of things on the agenda. This is not
one's purpose. This is a list of goals. Purpose is the guiding star
that makes you aspire to something greater, keeps you pointed in
the right direction, and helps simplify your life from being loaded
down with over-activity. The classic office sign of rajasic mode
says, "The hurrier I go, the behinder I get." In that case, the thing
to do is to slow down, get off the gerbil wheel long enough to
become quiet, and orient yourself to knowing your purpose, not
just goals. Why have you taken incarnation? While achieving goals
is necessary, why are you here? You may find there are a lot of
activities you are doing that have nothing to do with why you are
here; in fact, this busyness actually keeps you from accomplishing
essential things in your life.

The sattvic way moves you toward the mark. The body and
mind slow down; alert calmness allows you to tune in to your
soul's purpose: a purpose that comes from a very deep part of
you. When you tap into this, you simply know that it has been
true for you from before you were born. Purpose is inspiring,
life-giving, and in accomplishing it, you truly know that you will
feel profound satisfaction. There will not be a thousand of such
purposes in your life; there will be comparatively few. Your purpose may connect with a profession, family, and children, some
service to do in life, the perfection of some art or creative

endeavor, or purpose can relate to physical achievements such as a sport or perfect health. Purpose can relate to any topic at all, but it must rise to the standard of being connected with the real reason you were born.

Purpose uplifts any activity you are engaged in when it is aligned with why you are here. For instance, if being in service to God is your purpose, then going to a work in which you see yourself serving God in your customer or seeing the useful role that your product plays in people's lives, elevates any beneficial work that is dharmic into seva—loving service to others. All activities, including sweeping the floor, washing dishes, driving somewhere, educating yourself—any and all activities in alignment with purpose make the activity worthy and fulfilling.

Please take some time. Focus on the purpose you do know. How are you doing staying on track with that purpose? Also, check in with your deeper Self—is there any unacknowledged purpose you do not yet consciously acknowledge, or you have been pushing into the background? The first thing to do is to discover your true purpose in life—first things first! Every life has a purpose, even if your body does not cooperate in any other way, your purpose can be to be a prayer warrior for God. As such, you see every person, every situation in life filled with God's light and life, working towards His perfection. Your light can extend out all over this whole world, and even beyond. That is a mighty purpose!

I know that my purpose is to fulfill what God and Gurus have asked me to do: to love and serve Him and Him in you—writing this posting is in keeping with that purpose. Another purpose is to publish Mother's words in books and formats that are fitting to her work. That is a work in progress, and we are making good headway on that front. Another purpose is to be in perfect harmony with the body through eating the right foods in the correct amounts; to have no impediments to the flow of life-energy through this body; and for the intelligence of God to manifest through this brain. Every day, this is an exciting exploration.

An overarching purpose is to be a perfect instrument for God in thought, word, and action—to be in keeping with His will every moment of every day. This, you might say, is my meta-purpose in life. I find all of these stated purposes absolutely true for me; they are all inspiring and are polestars that keep me tremendously enthusiastic about life and in forward motion, rising to higher levels every day—it does not get better than that.

Your challenge is to be clear with your purpose and to be exactly on track with achieving it. So that when it comes time to draw your last breath, you may say, along with the Christ, "Father into thy hands I commend my spirit" (Luke 24:36), and then, "It is finished" (John 19:30). You know that you have completed the purpose for which you have taken incarnation; you feel in perfect accord with Divine Will, and can, in all good conscience, commend yourself to the highest light of your Being—that is what the Infinite has desired for you from the foundation of time.

February 8

WHERE TWO OR MORE ARE GATHERED

Jesus in the Temple, painting by Heinrich Hofmann, 1881.

O ne day, God gave me a funny. He said, "Where two or more are gathered . . . . There shall be politics." And you know, He is right! Because even amongst like-minded personalities, there will be differences on any topic when you get into particulars. Now, my mother told me not to discuss politics or religion in polite company, "It does no good." Well, that leaves what . . . ? The weather? Even that is not a safe subject today with global warming being such a hot topic!

People have differences; it is systemic to creation and to God's great diversity throughout nature. The word "politics" traces its history back to a book with that title written by Aristotle. After writing a book about ethics, his narrative naturally wove into his next book on politics. The Greek word "politikos" became the French word "politiques" and was later anglicized as "politics"—among its many shades of meaning is: "of, for, or relating to citizens."

Politics has always had its contentious side. When Julius Caesar proclaimed himself dictator, Marcus Brutus made his political point with the end of a knife to divest his old friend and mentor of his monarchical powers. With the death of millions of innocents along with the perpetrators down through the years, we definitely know there are real-life consequences to politics. Today, our airwaves are filled with raucous politics: sharp edges dueling and colliding with contrasting ideas and motivations. We are fortunate today that the majority of those sharp edges are words and not blades, guns, or worse.

And how do politics and spiritual living go together? In a word, carefully. There are those who tie religion and politics closely together, saying that God is on their side and those who do not agree are evil. And others make political assertions with all the certitude of religious conviction: dissenters are seen as immoral. In both cases, anyone differing from the "party line" is beyond respectable. There are real-life consequences to decisions made in the political arena, so it is easy to see why emotions can take over, and that is especially true when there is no respect for the God in another—seeing God in another even when he or she may be in error.

In the Mahabharata, the epic poem that includes an immense war, one of the warriors is asked, "Can you fight without anger?" This is an interesting question when the stakes are so high. He replies that he can. Only then is he allowed to enter into the fray. Inflamed emotions such as anger, greed, revenge, and fear can all lead to adharmic behavior that not only retards the progress of an individual, but all those his or her life touches. Therefore, those called to a political life are tested on their own unique battlefield and are called upon to act with the utmost integrity—to ever abide by their highest Light and for the greatest good of all.

And for those of us not directly on this battlefield, but interested participants in the body politic? We too must act in accordance with dharma. The very same emotions that sink a politician can be a black mark on a citizen. Explosive anger, fear, and greed leave their residue on any wayward devotee. Trust in God, compassion, and recognizing that good people can disagree, are ways to stay attuned to inward stillness and true wisdom. Master admonishes, "Wise men discuss, fools argue." Of course, all may have clear, well-defined positions, and many of us do, but keeping proper perspective is a must for spiritual balance.

Some choose to defer decisions to others and not get involved, but actively informed citizen-yogis help keep things on track. One does not need to watch every thrust and blow in hand-to-hand political combat, but to stay abreast of the evolving issues and tune into how God directs you on each issue is consistent with being a responsible citizen with the privilege to vote. This makes for a better, albeit imperfect, system.

Devotees too have widely varying perspectives on issues. Even this can lead to wonderful results. Two dear devotees are an example of this. One devotee has been a long-term activist for worker rights and the downtrodden. Another is a leader of a police force near the Canadian/American border. There was to be a large protest at the border crossing. The policeman arrived at a planning meeting between law enforcement and the protest organizers. He was anxious about the coming protest, knowing that they could take ugly turns. When he walked into the meeting, he recognized one of the organizers on the other side, a fellow kriyaban, an activist-friend; he immediately relaxed and thought, "Everything is going to be okay." And it was.

In God, every difference need not separate us in Spirit. Rather, first, find the unity operating beneath the great diversity of creation. As Jesus originally said, "Where two or three are gathered together in my name, there am I in the midst of them" (Matthew 18:20). Being established in this unity found in God-consciousness allows for the unfoldment of harmonious differences. Each one may hold firm opinions, yet there is a recognition that it is all God's play, and that God enjoys His play. God within you chooses your level of interest and involvement in the rough-and-tumble world of politics, but whatever He chooses for you, you are always mindful that this is theater; underneath, all are actors playing parts. By not losing contact with God, you do not get lost in the play.

February 10

LO, I AM WITH YOU ALWAYS

Jesus Tempted, painting by Carl Bloch, 1850.**

Greetings from the Southwest desert. We are currently encamped near Yuma, Arizona. An unfortunate consequence of this area is that we have enough cell tower connection to send and receive emails but not enough to stream live. It makes it difficult to listen when the broadcast stalls or loses total connection during a talk. So, today, we will commune in spirit: using our built-in inner-net.

You know, it truly is amazing what capacities we have that are too often unexplored. There are airwaves from radio and television bandwidths all around us, but we are not properly attuned to listen to or see such broadcasts. For that, we need a radio or television with the proper receiver. There are also subatomic particles flying right through us, even through the earth at incredible speeds, yet all of this goes unnoticed. As these things are going on around and through us (even as we read this).

A solar flare from our distant sun can interfere with a radio broadcast here on Earth, and so does the static of restless thoughts and ceaseless activity make hearing subtle communications between people unheard. One of the beautiful things about life in the astral worlds is that thought transference occurs naturally without misinterpreted words getting in the way. Even as writing is a poor substitute for a perfect memory, spoken words are a poor imitation of thought transference.

During my stay at Anandashram in 1998–1999, I sat each evening with Swamiji. He and a few intimates would go about ashram business while I quietly entered and sat next to the wall and meditated. He tolerated my presence without giving me the boot, so I would sit for an hour, then quietly pronam and leave. Often, while I was meditating with my eyes closed, I would know when his attention shifted to me; he did not call out to me, but I sensed it. I would open my eyes and he would be quietly waiting, then he would begin to talk to me. Now, if I had been more advanced, perhaps the conversation would have occurred without words at all; for this, too, has happened on more than one occasion.

There are those who try to develop psychic abilities, but the psychic realm is of a different nature than this deeper spiritual communion. The psychic realm can be used for many reasons, not necessarily for pure spiritual intent. After meeting Mother, I read the *Autobiography of a Yogi* every spring for ten years. It seemed like a good time of year for new seeds to be sown. I was amazed at the things I found in that same book with each reading. New information and new themes revealed themselves as if brand new with each reading. One year, a principle became crystal clear. Whenever a truly realized master performs a "miracle,"

Babaji, Lahiri Mahasaya, Sri Yukteswarji, or a highly realized saint, he or she announces that this extraordinary event was initiated by God's command. By God's command—not a whim, not for personal gain or to prove something—the purity of intent was from the highest Source.

When we go through the successive layers of human potential during our spiritual unfoldment, many temptations come to us: some are as subtle as the breeze on a still day; others slam into us like a speeding dump truck. Things will happen: psychic experiences, and powers of various kinds, present themselves. Even as Jesus is picturesquely portrayed as being tempted by Satan to display powers, to gain power, name, and fame in the world, so are we tempted. We may not have a being with pointed ears all in red standing before us, but he may as well be. He stands before us with a silver platter, asking if he can interest us in any of his wares; all we need to do is bow down to him and we may take. Of course, we may even think such abilities are a sign of spiritual advancement! Tricky devil. We must exhibit the utmost integrity and surrender all such powers, knowing that to the sincere yogi, these are detours that will take us off a cliff, not to the mountaintop.

Communion in God makes a bond of one with another; not simply through personal psychic connection, but through the purity and disinterest of God-experience. Then, what is known is a transfer of the highest and best for everyone concerned. Such communication is uplifting, purifying, and edifying on every level. When the receiver of God-consciousness is switched on, we feel the pulse of Divine Life throughout all creation. We realize these spiritual rays have always been in and around us, only we did not have the eyes to see and the ears to hear (Matthew 13:43). Become an active receiver, and realize the universal truth of Jesus' reminder—that he is with us always. Let us go within and commune with our Infinite Beloved, and through Him, with all.

February 14

THE LOVE OF SAINT VALENTINE

Saint Valentine icon, c. 1496.

I want to wish you a lovely Valentine's Day, a day brimming with the love of God filling your heart to overflowing. According to early Christian history, Saint Valentine died a martyr, but while in prison, he healed the daughter of his jailor of blindness. When he wrote her a letter, he signed it, "Your Valentine." Saint Valentine not only forgave his jailor but healed his daughter—such a loving thing to do.

Master wrote so beautifully of charity. Charity has taken on different meanings down through time, from its original meaning of love, to acts of love, to helping someone in need, to non-profit organizations. But, let us examine the word from its headwaters, love and acts of love, as Master does:

> Charity is born of sympathy. By empathy, a quality of Omnipresence, a person may transfer his consciousness to that within suffering men and experience, as his own, their griefs and limitations. It is then that the charitable desire to offer help springs forth.
>
> Selfishness cramps the omnipresent soul in a miserable prison of limiting material desires. You should desire salvation so that you may give it to everyone else. You should desire to drink God's nectar of bliss so that you may share it with all. That is true charity.[17]

Master so beautifully connects the act of giving back to its source, Omnipresence, from which empathy naturally springs. In Omnipresence we feel what others feel; however, it is not a simple connection to another, rather, we take with us awareness of God's love and compassion as well as His clarity that helps us discern truth and right behavior. If someone is struggling with staying true to his or her higher Self, then, through an omnipresent state of witnessing, they can, if discerning, sense the future consequences of wrong actions, as can we on their behalf. Intuiting the suffering that individual will go through, our heart goes out to such a one. Whenever anyone suffers the effects of past actions in body, mind, or soul, we feel compassionate understanding for that one—we feel the fullness of God's love flowing through our own heart in omniscient empathy.

In seeing all creation as an expression of Ananda, God's bliss, then we see the truth, even as Saint Kabir did when he said, "I

---

17   Paramhansa Yogananda. Para-Gram card.

laugh when I hear that the fish in the water is thirsty."[18] [19] Truly, we swim in an ocean of love, an ocean of bliss; it is all around us, and we are immersed in it; we need only drink of what is so abundantly permeating the air we breathe.

And this is my Saint Valentine's wish for you, my dear One, that you may drink to your heart's content from the Living Waters of Spirit; that your heart may run full to overflowing with love for God and all creation. That, when you do an act of charity, it is first an act of love, an action that is a natural outcome of Omnipresence. And when you are the receiver of someone's loving act, that you receive the love behind the act and are conscious of it first. In this way, it is truly God giving to God. It is in that spirit that you please me most in receiving all the love of God that is overflowing from my heart and that I see flowing out to you now.

"Your Valentine."

---

18   *Songs of Kabir.* "I laugh when I hear that the fish in the water is thirsty. You don't grasp the fact that what is most alive of all is inside your own house; and you walk from one holy city to the next with a confused look." www.goodreads.com

19   *Songs of Kabir.* Here is another translation by Rabindranath Tagore: "I laugh when I hear that the fish in the water is thirsty: You do not see that the Real is in your home, and you wander from forest to forest listlessly! Here is the truth! Go where you will, to Benares, Mathura; if you do not find your soul, the world is unreal to you" (p. 74).

February 17

I MYSELF DO NOTHING

Shiva gives the heavenly weapon Pashupatastra to Arjuna,
a master of archery with a perfect focus of attention.**

Since my early twenties, two favorite scriptures have inspired me, stayed with me, and been my friends and guides these many years. The scriptures are the "New Testament" sayings of Jesus and the teachings of Krishna in the *Bhagavad Gita*. In terms of pure poetic imagery and concise Truth, these two Avatars are truly amazing. I have never made a study of either of these from an academic viewpoint; rather, I use them for inspiration. I may have read through them from beginning to end but a few times, if at all. I am much more likely to pick up the narrative at God's prompting and latch on to a few verses. Soon, I have the inspiration I need; my soul is lifted on these scriptural wings that elevate my consciousness and deliver me into Heavenly Realms; finally, my soul merges into Spirit; self becomes Self.

This morning, I pick up the Gita, and my eyes rest on this:

> The cognizer of truth, united to God, automatically perceives, "I myself do nothing"—even though he sees, hears, touches, smells, eats, moves, sleeps, breathes, speaks, rejects, holds, opens, or closes his eyes—realizing that it is the senses (activated by Nature) that work amid sense objects. Like unto the lotus leaf that remains unsullied by water, the yogi who performs actions, forswearing attachment and surrendering his actions to the Infinite, remains unbound by entanglement in the senses.[20]

There are times when it seems that Jesus is quoting Krishna; such as, when he says, "When ye have lifted up the Son of man, then shall ye know that I am he, and that I do nothing of myself; but as my Father hath taught me" (John 8:28).

Let us take this idea: It is not this "I" who acts. In fact, this "I" is what both Krishna and Jesus start with, "I do nothing." The "I" has gone through a change, from "the one acting" into being a witness of what is done. The "lifting up of the son of man" is the transformation that leads us from ego consciousness to being "united with God."

You may sense in yourself how fundamental this notion of doership is to your nature: "I am doing this, feeling this, thinking this." From a purely human standpoint, if you do not have this sense of being the doer, you are labeled with a dissociative disorder. However, feeling like you are disconnected from your body or its actions because of psychological trauma is not what

---

20   *Bhagavad Gita.* Chapter Five, verses 8–10.

is being described here. No, this state of consciousness comes as an earned experience it is an advancement in the psyche, not a setback.

You can begin to get an idea of this state by practicing being the witness to what you are doing. Many years ago, I read a book, *Zen in the Art of Archery*, By Eugen Herrigel. In it, he describes the discipline of the Zen monk watching himself go through all the motions of shooting a bow and arrow. Sounds easy enough. Nothing could be further from the truth. It takes years of practice, observing every movement of muscle, stringing the bow, setting the arrow, pulling the string, bending the bow, aiming at the target, and releasing the arrow. Everything is done with full mindfulness; without the mind wandering here and there, the mind must be totally focused on the action being performed. When done correctly, shooting a bow and arrow becomes a meditation; you are the witness; then something extraordinary happens: the Zen state of mind.

While reading this book, I decided to do my own kind of "witness" practice. When I was doing the simplest of tasks, I observed myself in the doing, every muscle being moved, the sensation of moving in space, sounds in the room, breathing, even the heart beating; everything was noted by the observer within. And what did I experience? Physically and mentally, I slowed down; I was aware of minute movements. And something more, my consciousness moved from the "doer" to the observer. The practice shifted me into a meditative state as the body continued in its action. It was very nice.

Through time and experience, this practice took on new dimensions, even though I was no longer practicing as inspired by the book. Rather, being the observer took on its own life. I felt that Prakriti (the power of Nature) was moving through me—prana, or life-force, was doing the work through this body. Then came another level of awareness: It is God, the supreme power and intelligence that is beyond Nature that is acting, speaking, and even thinking through this form.

I have to say, these are magnificent realizations to be had. They change your life, and if you let them, they transform you. The "son of man" in you is "lifted up;" you become the "cognizer of truth, united with God." In that union, you know in truth the statement, "I do nothing; it is my Heavenly Father who doeth the works" (John 14:10, adapted). Now, everything that is said and done through this form comes through the "I" witness from a much higher Source.

When an aspirant "lifts up" the human consciousness (the son of man) into the Divine Consciousness (our Heavenly Father), then the aspirant knows the same transformation, the same truth. Whatever happens to the body and the world becomes like water slipping off the "enameled leaf," leaving the inner Son of God ever in oneness with the Heavenly Father.

February 21

THE DEEP

A whale of inspiration.**

Dispassion is a topic that Krishna and yogi-saints return to frequently. In the *Bhagavad Gita*, we read:

> O mighty-armed Prince, undoubtedly the mind is fickle and unruly; but by yoga practice and by dispassion, O Arjuna, the mind may nevertheless be controlled.
>
> This is My word: Yoga is difficult of attainment by the ungoverned man; but he who is self-controlled will, by striving through proper methods, be able to achieve it.[21]

21   *Bhagavad Gita.* Chapter Six, verses 35–6.

As aspirants, it is important for us to understand this most potent word, dispassion (vairagya). We work toward Self-realization when we practice controlling our thoughts through Kriya Meditation. When circulating the life-force through the spine and brain, we discover a balance of mind in which we experience inner stillness. From this stillness, we are actively aware but the world of the senses seems one step removed. This naturally creates a state of dispassion.

We can compare this true inner state of dispassionate stillness with the yogi-aspirant who is practicing to be dispassionate. In this case, the aspirant is striving to rise above physical sensations, emotional states, and insistent thoughts, though not actively experiencing stillness; he or she is not yet above allowing the things of the world to disturb stillness.

When the mind thinks about projecting itself into a state of dispassion, it can think, "Oh, what a dull place to be," or, "I could never be indifferent to the world." Either we think we could not or would not want dispassion. However, this state of consciousness spoken of by Krishna and the saints is not only possible, it is to be much desired.

Look at it this way—let us imagine our consciousness stretching itself out to be a great ocean. We are the depths of that ocean; the waves are rolling on the surface, other currents are running deep like massive rivers throughout our oceanic self, various thermal layers are realms unto themselves, big and small fish and mammals are moving within us—we are the totality of all that the ocean is.

Now, the big and small waves on the surface are thoughts and sensations that exist for shorter or longer periods of time; the river currents are deeper wisdom-thoughts of God coursing throughout our being, and thermal layers are various levels of consciousness in us. All these aspects play and sport about in the totality of ourselves as the ocean, all coming and going.

We are aware of all these comings and goings; however, we are also aware of the deep nature of the ocean, of our identity as the ocean itself in which all these activities are taking place. It is not that these various aspects of ourselves are unreal, but none of them change The Deep in us—our Soul, Self, or Spirit. Imagine that we are aware of all the different parts at play, but whatever they do or do not do, they do not alter The Deep in us—the changeless and ever-existent part of us.

In our spiritual practice, we can, and it is beneficial to, work on being dispassionate towards the things of the world. You can keep the image of being identified with the vast Deep of the ocean as a helpful mental practice. At the same time, we are aware of the alternating waves of experiences that pass over our surface, but never distress or disturb The Deep in us. Then, through our continued sadhana, we experience a momentous shift in awareness: we are no longer imagining The Deep, we become identified with it. We actively see the things of the world playing on the surface of our consciousness, each part having its time of existence, but not altering The Deep in us.

Gradually, we are permanently established in The Deep. Now worldly-experience is seen as passing phenomena but we never exclusively identify with it. We realize that The Deep is our true Self, and that we are ever That. We are no longer practicing dispassion. We have become dispassion itself. All that is in the ocean exists in us: the thought-wave sense experiences, the deep-diving whales of revelation, the thermal layers of consciousness, and the broad river currents of intuitive wisdom from God roll over our surface and move through us. Each is created, preserved for a time, and then it disappears back into us once again. All the while, we are ever at one with The Deep. We know that we are the great "I Am That I Am" in the beginningless, endless, ocean of Self.

February 24

THE LEAVENED BREAD

Mother Hamilton, Los Angeles, mid-1970s.**

A nother parable spake he unto them, "The kingdom of heaven is like unto leaven, which a woman took, and hid in three measures of meal, till the whole was leavened" (Matthew 13:33).

And what does this saying mean? The leaven is a substance that makes the bread rise. And what is that yeast in us that makes us rise up to the kingdom of heaven? The spiritual master sows a seed in the aspirant, the power of God in the master warms the "oven" of consciousness for that one, making the conditions right; for "the whole is leavened." The "three measures" are for the three bodies: the physical, astral, and causal.

The guru ignites a fire in the devotee that results in focused sadhana. Ongoing spiritual practice, done with intensity, makes the "oven warm." This warmth allows the bread to keep rising and rising as the consciousness is experiencing more upliftment: more God-experience. And what happens if the oven cools? If the aspirant loses the fire of renunciation and a glowing love for God? Then, the bread will cease rising and will collapse in on itself once again.

When I met Mother, I felt such a power of God coming from her. She focused my mind on chanting God's name. She initiated me into the practice of Kriya Yoga. She gave me the means to make the interior consciousness glow—the bread to rise. However, this did not happen in an instant. In the beginning, God-experience came a little here and a little there. My desire for God was strong but so were the opposing forces. It continued to be a tremendous battle.

We should not imagine that all we have to do is to reach out for God and we will have everything. Mother describes God-realization as the "pearl of great price," and indeed it is! No one can read about the life of Jesus, in whose footsteps we are told to follow, and think it all happens in a day and without the greatest commitment. Even while being aware of these difficulties, it must be balanced with knowing that we have wonderful examples of accomplished yogis and spiritual masters who demonstrate what is possible; that we too might know God.

What love I have had for sitting on my meditation blanket with mala beads in hand. Feeling the sacred Kriya Breath revolving in the spine and brain, making me feel close to our guru-lineage, being purified from the inside out. Every morning and night spent in the laboratory of my own body and soul. I learn to explore inner depths and heights of consciousness, feeling deepening peace, inner stillness, and a growing awareness of the Divine Presence. All of this—warming the oven.

It is easiest to speak about extraordinary experiences; what is more difficult to describe is the comfort and glow of joy that comes from engaging in deepened meditation. A smile grows through inner radiance, love glows in my heart, and peace is felt within and without; these are signs of being on the right track.

A favorite quote of mine from Sri Yukteswarji in the *Autobiography of a Yogi*:

> My guru was smiling. "I am sure you aren't expecting a venerable Personage, adorning a throne in some antiseptic corner of the cosmos! I see, however, that you are imagining that the possession of miraculous powers is knowledge of God. One might have the whole universe, and find the Lord elusive still! Spiritual advancement is not measured by one's outward powers, but only by the depth of his bliss in meditation. Ever-new Joy is God. He is inexhaustible; as you continue your meditations during the years, He will beguile you with an infinite ingenuity. Devotees like yourself who have found the way to God never dream of exchanging Him for any other happiness; He is seductive beyond thought of competition. How quickly we weary of earthly pleasures! Desire for material things is endless; man is never satisfied, completely, and pursues one goal after another. The 'something else' he seeks is the Lord, who alone can grant lasting joy."[22]

When we sit for meditation, let us take with us our remembrance of our connection with saints and realized masters from the world over as we plug into the Creator of all that is. What a sacred privilege this is. In the depths of our meditation, we are fulfilling what we have come to do. In the peace and joy of

---

22   *Autobiography of a Yogi* (pp. 98–9).

communion with God, the oven warms and the bread rises as we enter our kingdom of heaven.

❋   ❋   ❋

Travel Note: We are currently encamped at Picacho Peak State Park, Arizona. It is lovely here with Saguaro Cactus, rugged hills, and rock formations all around. Although not the frigid temperatures experienced throughout much of America, we had snow on peaks the other day and it has rained a good deal. It has been a cold desert, although scheduled to get warmer this week. Yesterday, I was taken out for a pre-birthday lunch at a restaurant in Tucson that Carla and I went to three years ago and remembered still for its delicious food and good service. We gathered there and it was a perfect time of celebration. We will continue camping here until this coming Friday. Blessings

Launch of a birthday season!

Birthday Celebration: Yogacharya David and Carla,
with Jerry and Lois Hickenbottom, Rick and Judy Ellis,
and Corliss Harmer, Tucson, Arizona, 2019.

February 26

BEST JOB, EVER

Yogacharya David at Grand Tetons National Park, 2016.**

First thing this morning, Carla wished me a happy birthday, a very fine thing. The first thought I have on hearing this is that the person who should be honored on my birthday is my mother. She is the one who carried me around for nine months while chasing after my two brothers: morning sickness, her body having to accommodate a nine-plus pound child growing in her, going through birth pains and a 10 p.m. delivery—a long day, I am sure. Because I had been breech, she had sutures and was in pain and needed help for a few weeks afterward from my aunt Joyce who was in school at the time. And me? I was just along for the ride throughout all of this—that is, until a rude awakening of being born into this world with its brightly-lit room and a welcoming slap to get the breathing started. Welcome to the new world!

I was the third of three, a few years after my brothers. When I asked my mother if I was unplanned, she said, "No." When I asked if she had been hoping for a girl, she said, "No," she was happy with whatever I was. I never believed her about not hoping for a girl, but I think it was a justifiable lie. She had grown up an only girl, and I think she may have wondered what she ever did to deserve getting three active boys to raise. In our adulthood, two of the best days of the year for my mom were Thanksgiving and Christmas, when all her children and then grandchildren, and ultimately great-grandchildren, were all there. Yes, she certainly deserves to be honored today.

This early morning, Saturn is bright, but Venus is truly blazing on the forehead of the eastern sky. The Big Dipper stands mighty, always pointing us to the North Star for direction, and Orion's belt and sword ever remind me of Arjuna, the faithful warrior on the spiritual battlefield. It is a brisk cold day with gusty winds and the screen-monitor sky has gradually brightened, revealing a saguaro cactus forest all around and craggy peaks on either side. It is a good day to be alive.

There are two great joys in my life right now. The first is to see aspirants with both feet on the path: striving, working, loving, and giving heart, mind, and soul to the Divine Quest. And not just that, but showing signs of progress: skin shining, eyes glittering, bliss, and love filling their cups to overflowing. It is not that every day we must look like a front-page cover for Enlightenment Today, not when there are dark nights to be endured and heavy burdens that must be carried. But a general trend upward. What started as a spark, then became a flame, and is now, our aim, a blazing sun of aspiration. In my soul, I walk with each one God has given me; I slog through the muck, I strain at the climb, and I glory in newfound vistas with each one of you. It is my greatest privilege to share in the toils but also to stand alongside you on glorious peaks of realization. It is the best of lives, the noblest of goals, and the most fulfilling of accomplishments to go to God together.

My second great joy in life is that Mother has given me some tasks to do for her. It has been one of God's precious jokes in life for Him to assign me the task of assembling Mother's prodigious compilation of spoken words, making them into book form. Me, who worked harder in high school studies to get out of work than simply doing the work. Me, who spends many hours writing a posting that is read in minutes. Me, who knew more about sin than syntax in high school; this is who God assigns this work to? Fine joke, Ram!

Not only that, but He has me writing to you in these postings, and other publications, as well as working on Mother's writings. I am reassured by God that even a broken candle can still give light. If so, it is only because of God and Gurus' blessings that anything of note may be done through this form. I am also blessed with those who did pay attention in English class as part of our virtual International Headquarters of the Cross and Lotus Publishing, to keep me from complete embarrassment.

So, I think I have absolutely the best job description in the world. When the timer for this body is up, my greatest wish is that God and Gurus may give even the smallest indication that they are at all pleased with the work done here in their names. It is truly a bold proclamation to say that I work for God and Gurus, but it is not without justification. Mother gave me this work; she is a product of her master, as he was of his own master, and I know that God has given His stamp upon my Soul, and, in this, I have complete assurance that I am "about my Father's business" (Luke 2:49).

Now, it is up to me to utilize each day for His glory and to manifest His Light through all that I think, do, and say. It is the greatest joy that we may go to God together. He blesses us so that each of us fulfills the tasks He has given. In saying this as my birthday wish, I do not blow out the lit candle, but I ask that lighted souls everywhere may manifest more and more light for the One, and for all.

March 2

Lessons of a Mediator

White lotus.**
"Blessed are the peacemakers . . . " (Matthew 5:9).

My years as a mediator—volunteering as a mediator, working as a trainer for the first Dispute Resolution Center in Washington State, and serving as a founding principal in Conflict Resolution Service—brought forth a time of extremely rich experiences and learning. A mediator is a bit like a firefighter who runs into a flaming building that everyone else is running away from!

Becoming a mediator was a big journey for me since beforehand I tended to be a conflict avoider. So, the idea of changing directions, and heading for the fire, was contrary to everything I knew up until that time. However, with new tools in hand, mediation gave me an opportunity to learn a number of lessons about conflict and human nature. Here are some things I learned along the way.

First Lesson: **The power of "I'm sorry."** Something as fundamental as what your mother taught you does wonders in a conflict—a simple and sincere apology, "I am sorry." During discussions that involved thousands or tens of thousands of dollars, the fate of careers, and the happiness of whole neighborhoods, a sincere apology worked wonders to resolve conflicts—negotiations most often went smoothly after a climactic apology.

Lesson Two: **What is being fought over is rarely what is really at issue**. People argue over money, children, and all sorts of other things. But what is usually driving the demands people make when taking a hard position is something that is not being said: disappointment, identity, safety, or values. Attachment to an expectation is a very powerful thing; "I thought you were going to . . . " The hurt and anger over disappointment definitely fuels the feud. The key? Go behind the scenes to discover: "Why is this thing you are asking for so important to you?" Find that out, and then you can talk about how to address the underlying interest, instead of arguing over intractable positions.

Lesson Three: **Conflicts are costly**. When people take hard positions and make demands, it is good to explore, "What is the "cost" of this ongoing conflict?" We can be myopic when hurt or angry and take a stubborn position that ends up hurting us more by prolonging a conflict. Do a quick calculation: what is the cost of hurting others in terms of money, resources, lost time, emotional energy, stress, legal consequences, and diminished opportunities? The cost can be varied and enormous, but you are too invested in keeping angry vengeance or fearful avoidance to take time to add up the cost. Oftentimes, laying out the cost upfront helps you to understand it is in your best interest to work for a solution.

Lesson Four: **The benefits of civility**. One of the responsibilities of a mediator is to keep the discussion between disputants civil and productive. Truth need not be a casualty of being respectful—in fact, it is far more likely what one side is saying will be heard by the other party when spoken with respect. Ungoverned anger, both in words and actions, can immediately derail any progress toward finding a solution. Then, there are people who use anger as a way to intimidate and win. Neither uncontrolled anger nor being a bully will work to find a long-term, satisfying resolution. Speaking the truth with respect is the quickest way to be heard by another and to resolve a conflict.

Lesson Five: **Emotions balloon up and make problems bigger**. Emotions can balloon up—anger, hurt, and resentment can take on huge proportions, especially when something has festered for a long time. The "emotional balloon" needs to deflate to a reasonable size in order for it to not carry things away to unknown, uncertain, and worse places than where you started. Taking time to get some perspective by talking it out confidentially with a friend or working it out of the body through exercise are two ways to decrease the emotional balloon. Then you can talk calmly about what is most important to the one with whom you are having differences.

Lesson Six: **Avoidance makes conflict worse**. My good friend and mediator Paul says, "Go to the heat." The heat is what most people avoid, but that is where the life-energy is. Many have been burned by heat, so tend to avoid it. However, learning to use the heat to find truth and unlock its life-energy for productive use will create new associations in your mind about what can happen through conflict resolution. Now, you can be excited to unlock new and positive possibilities when all that life-energy is directed to create something that will be good for everyone. It is fine to take some time to deflate your emotional balloon; that is a very useful thing to do. But do not let the opportunity slip away for working through a knotty problem. When you and the other party are ready, then use your skills and go to the heat!

Lesson Seven: **Good faith is a must: "It takes two to dance."** In any conflict, there will be at least two parties involved. For a voluntary resolution, whoever is involved needs to be there in good faith. That does not mean they know something positive is going to happen in advance, but they sincerely want a resolution to the conflict. One of the few failed mediations I conducted was a landlord-tenant conflict. The tenant was behind in rent, and the landlord was willing to be flexible but felt things had gone on too long. In a caucus during a confidential meeting, the tenant told me that the only reason she agreed to mediation was to buy more time for staying in her apartment. She had no intention of paying her rent. I could not tell the landlord what she had said, but I called an immediate end to the mediation due to the fact that not all parties were there in good faith. Sincerity is required in order to find common ground that will create a solution that works for everyone.

Lessons in being proactive. You can work to keep differences from growing into an oversized conflict by proactively practicing the above principles. When you realize you have made a mistake, make a sincere apology. Work to understand what is really going on under the surface when you or someone else is upset or makes demands. Then, speak to that underlying issue. Also, recognize the cost of conflict; it absolutely takes a toll. Keeping the cost in mind will motivate you to address the problem and work it out. And, for goodness' sake, be civil; it is one of life's great inventions—being respectful can often stop a conflict before it starts. Then, before you address a conflict, be sure you have let some of the air out of your stretched emotional balloon before you say or do something that destroys the fabric of your relationship with another. When there is a conflict, work to resolve it; don't avoid it. Taking time to cool down is good, but do not let the topic go cold. And, at all times, be sincere in your dealings with others—good faith is required to find good solutions.

These are the lessons that I have learned about conflict through helping hundreds of people resolve some very tough, seemingly intractable, problems. These lessons have been valuable to me. Resolve to be a peacemaker in your life and help this world to be a better place for yourself and others.

"Blessed are the peacemakers: for they shall be called the children of God" (Matthew 5:9).

March 7

MASTER HEARS OUR SOUL'S WHISPERS

Paramhansa Yogananda, *The Last Smile*, 1952.**

Here, we have from Dr. Lewis a firsthand account of his experiences with Master just days before his leaving the body. Dr. Lewis gave this talk three days after Master's Mahasamadhi:

Now I'll tell you one or two things about my own experiences with him [during] the last few days. Lately, he had been reminiscing about how we started way back in Boston, 32 years ago. He said, "Remember Electric Avenue?" That's where we used to live. "All the good times we used to have?" And I said, "Yes." And he said,

"We've had a good life, haven't we?" I said, "That's right." I said, "Yes, we might have been hanging around a night club and things like that. But no. This is better. We can let go." Then he said quickly, without much emphasis, "We'll be parted for a little while and then we'll be together again." But the delusion was so great that even then I wouldn't accept it. I knew my soul went just right back when he said it. Sure, the Lord keeps it covered up pretty well.

When he said we'd be separated for a little bit but then together again, then he said right at that time, I remember so distinctly, "But remember, I'll be closer to you when I'm out of this body, than I have been in the body." So, remember, there is the key. So let us not be depressed. Let us not feel bad. God is running the show. We are His children, and His Infinite Light is with us. In that Light is the master and all great saints. There is nothing to fear except if we do not stay in that Light and Consciousness. That's all.

And so, I feel better. A load has been lifted. I didn't know what the load was, with some physical trouble going with it. But the load was that coming events cast their shadow, and the Soul knows it. And so be of good cheer. The Master is not away from us. He is with us more, and more.

Master's Last Evening

Master was scheduled to give a speech welcoming the new Ambassador from India during a banquet at the Biltmore Hotel in Los Angeles. What a fulfillment, an Ambassador from a free India! The freedom movement led by Mahatma Gandhi, whom Master had met and initiated into Kriya Yoga; a freedom movement that came with definite birth pains but was at last a reality—that Master had lived long enough to see it become a reality. The new Ambassador and his wife had come to a luncheon put on by Master, and they all got on famously.

The night of the banquet Master had reserved a room at the Biltmore to rest beforehand. He had been carrying a terrific load in his body, enduring so much pain, heart problems and difficulty in walking. He said that Divine Mother had scheduled that he leave his body well before this time, but he had prayed for more time so he could complete his commentary on the Bhagavad Gita—which he did and pronounced that it was ready to publish.

This is what Dr. Lewis said during that same talk about Master's physical condition in his last years (remember Master was only in his fifties at the time):

And then, from then on it was a terrific fight. For a long, long time he just laid there. Because you cannot take the karma of thousands of people, thousands of people, without a reaction—that's the spiritual law. It is not ordinary sickness. People make that mistake. It is because he takes the sins and the karma of others. And he has told me two things which were a direct result of the taking of karma of others. One was the condition of his legs. The other was the condition of his heart.

And so, from then on, for months he lay without moving. Gradually, up and walking about. He said many times, "I have no interest." He said, "It's only a few little things I have to make myself want to enjoy the senses," and so forth. "But," he said, "for a few of you, I stay." Now these are facts.

Even though he endured so much suffering in his body, he continued to move the world toward God. So, he attended the banquet, and when you see his picture known as "the last smile," taken that evening, you would never guess he was ready to leave the body, he radiates so much light, love, and divinity.

Master stood to talk, the room quieted, and he gave a lively, funny, and heartfelt talk. He told a favorite story about when he first arrived in America. He had heard about Native Americans scalping white men, and when he saw a number of bald men walking about, he thought with horror that the Indians must have been at work! Then, he concluded his talk with a recitation of his poem, "My India:"

Hail, mother of religions, lotus, scenic beauty,
And sages!
Thy wide doors are open,
Welcoming God's true sons through all ages.
Where Ganges, woods, Himalayan caves, and men dream God—
I am hallowed; my body touched that sod.

Ah, as Master concluded this poem, he felt himself leaving the body. He turned to his right. The traditional way for a yogi's mahasamadhi is to rotate to the right three times. But, as usual, Master was in a rush when it came to God, and he only started his first turn when he dropped his body—flying to his eternal freedom in God, flying to the feet of his dearest Guru, flying into the spiritual arms of his Infinite Beloved.[23]

---

23   http://ocoy.org/yoganandas-last-days/

Master was not "taken away;" rather, he is now permeating every particle of space, in every flower's fragrance and in the golden sunset. Even closer, he is in your heart and can be heard in your soul's whispers. Master is ever with the attuned soul, ever waiting for you to follow him into your eternal oneness with your Heavenly Father and Divine Mother.

Editor's Note: We have included a reflection from Paramhansa Yogananda; words that reflect what Yogacharya David taught as an overall truth: soul-intuition: staying in touch with one's deep inner core of Truth. Here, in *The Second Coming of Christ*, Master is speaking about Nicodemus, a seeker of deeper wisdom.

> . . . anyone can contact that [heavenly] Source and know the wonders that proceed therefrom, even as Jesus himself did, by undergoing the spiritual "second birth" of intuitional soul-awakening. The superficially curious crowds attracted by displays of phenomenal powers received only scantily from the wisdom trove of Jesus, but the manifest sincerity of Nicodemus elicited from the Master determined guidance that emphasized the supreme Power and Goal on which man should concentrate.
>
> Miracles of wisdom to enlighten the mind are superior to miracles of physical healing and the subjugation of nature; and the even greater miracles is the healing of the root-cause of every form of suffering: delusive ignorance that obscures the unity of man's soul and God. That primordial forgetfulness is vanquished only be Self-realization, through the intuitive power by which the soul directly apprehends its own nature as individualized Spirit and perceives spirit as the essence of everything.
>
> All bona fide revealed religions of the world are based on intuitive knowledge. Each has an exoteric or outer

peculiarity, and an esoteric or inner core. The exoteric is the public image, and includes moral precepts and a body of doctrines, dogmas, dissertations, rules, and customs to guide the general populace of its followers. The esoteric aspect includes methods that focus on actual communion of the soul with God. The exoteric aspect is for many; the esoteric is for the ardent few. It is the esoteric aspect of the religion that leads to intuition, the firsthand knowledge of Reality.

The lofty *Sanatama Dharma* of the Vedic philosophy of ancient India—summarized in the Upanishads and in the six classical systems of metaphysical knowledge, and peerlessly encapsulated in the *Bhagavad Gita*—is based on intuitional perception of the Transcendental Reality. Buddhism, with its various methods of controlling the mind and gaining depth in meditations, advocates intuitive knowledge to realize the transcendence of nirvana. Sufism in Islam anchors on the intuitive mystical experience of the soul. Within Jewish religion are esoteric teachings based on inner experience of the Divine, evidenced abundantly in the legacy of the God-illumined Biblical prophets. Christ's teachings are fully expressive of that realization. The apostle John's Revelation is a remarkable disclosure of the soul's intuitional; perception of deepest truths garbed in metaphor.[24]

---

24   (pp. 239–240).

March 9

SRI YUKTESWARJI'S MAHASAMADHI

Sri Yukteswarji and Paramhansa
Yogananda, Calcutta, India, 1935.**
Today is the anniversary of Sri Yukteswariji's
Mahasamadhi on March 9, 1936.

A nniversary of Sri Yukteswarji Mahasamadhi—March 9,
1936.

The *Autobiography of a Yogi,* by Paramhansa Yogananda,
is an amazingly told story on so many levels, written by such a
tremendous soul. Master, a yogi of great realization, did not try
to pose as "above it all;" rather, he gave us a picture of how he
suffered the pangs of shock and depression at the passing of his

own Master—it created a darkened night for him. Master wrote in the Autobiography:

> "Come to Puri ashram at once." This telegram was sent on March 8th by a brother disciple to Atul Chandra Roy Chowdhry, one of Master's chelas from Calcutta. News of the message reached my ears; anguished at its implications, I dropped to my knees and implored God that my guru's life be spared. As I was about to leave Father's home for the train, a divine voice spoke within.
>
> "Do not go to Puri tonight. Thy prayer cannot be granted."
>
> "Lord," I said, grief-stricken, "Thou dost not wish to engage with me in a 'tug of war' at Puri, where Thou wilt have to deny my incessant prayers for Master's life. Must he, then, depart for higher duties at Thy behest?"
>
> In obedience to the inward command, I did not leave that night for Puri. The following evening, I set out for the train; on the way, at seven o'clock, a black astral cloud suddenly covered the sky. Later, while the train roared toward Puri, a vision of Sri Yukteswar appeared before me. He was sitting, very grave at countenance, with a light on each side.
>
> "Is it all over?" I lifted my arms beseechingly.
>
> He nodded, then slowly vanished. As I stood on the Puri train platform the following morning, still hoping against hope, an unknown man approached me.
>
> "Have you heard that your master is gone?" He left me without another word; I never discovered who he was nor how he had known where to find me. Stunned, I swayed against the platform wall, realizing that in diverse ways my guru was trying to convey to me the devastating news. Seething with rebellion, my soul was like a volcano.

By the time I reached the Puri hermitage, I was nearing collapse. The inner voice was tenderly repeating "Collect yourself. Be calm."

I entered the ashram room where Master's body, unimaginably lifelike, was sitting in the lotus posture—a picture of health and loveliness. A short time before his passing, my guru had been slightly ill with fever, but before the day of his ascension into the infinite, his body had become completely well. No matter how often I looked at his dear form, I could not realize that its life had departed. His skin was smooth and soft; in his face was a beatific expression of tranquility. He had consciously relinquished his body at the hour of mystic summoning.

"The Lion of Bengal is gone!" I cried in a daze.[25]

After returning to Calcutta, Master continues:

My days were filled with lectures, classes, interviews, and reunions with old friends. Beneath a hollow smile and a life of ceaseless activity, a stream of black brooding polluted the inner river of bliss which for so many years had meandered under the sands of all my perceptions.[26]

In his letters to Rajasi, he expands on the grief that filled him at that time. He wrote this letter on March 17th while he was at Ranchi, just days after his guru's passing. Here is an excerpt:

If there were words, I would write to you how I feel about the material disappearance of Master. Imagine, the

---

25 *Autobiography of a Yogi* (pp. 394–5). Editor's Note: This dialogue is a replacement for Yogacharya David's original, due to copyright restrictions.

26 (p. 396).

Lord God did not want me to pray lest He have to grant my prayer or deny it. The lion has left his cage, the lion whose roar of wisdom kept me undergoing a thousand privations and demands of organization work. If I could weep, I would feel relieved. If I would cry, the gods would cry with me. If I had a thousand mouths, I would say India lost one of the greatest in wisdom. But the saddest of all is I could not show him you.[27]

We can all relate to, at least to some extent, the sense of loss and sadness Master was feeling at the passing of his master. What is amazing is how open Master is with his feelings, with no pretense that he is undisturbed. He puts a human face on being God-realized. For, even as Mother, he was both fully human and fully divine.

As much as he had grieved, so did he feel the intensity of joy at his guru's resurrection. Again, from the Autobiography:

Gone was the sorrow of parting. The pity and grief for his death, long robber of my peace, now fled in stark shame. Bliss poured forth like a fountain through endless, newly opened soul-pores. Anciently clogged with disuse, they now widened in purity at the driving flood of ecstasy. Subconscious thoughts and feelings of my past incarnations shed their karmic taints, lustrously renewed by Sri Yukteswar's divine visit.[28]

When I sat meditating at Puri's Samadhi Temple during my 1998 pilgrimage, I unexpectedly felt Sri Yukteswar's joy in torrents. Sri Yukteswarji made me know that his promise to his disciple,

---

27   *Rajarsi Janakananda: A Great Western Yogi* (p. 6).

28   *Autobiography of a Yogi* (p. 416).

recorded in the Autobiography, was not just for Paramhansaji, but for all of us:

> "Dearest Master! Rebuke me a million times—do scold me now!"
>
> "I shall chide you no more." His divine voice was grave, yet with an undercurrent of laughter. "You and I shall smile together, so long as our two forms appear different in the maya-dream of God. Finally, we shall merge as one in the Cosmic Beloved; our smiles shall be His smile, our unified song of joy vibrating throughout eternity to be broadcast to God-tuned souls!"[29]

It is good to remember that God-realized souls live human lives; they endure what everyone goes through at one time or another. They do this to show us that our humanness is not a bar to experiencing God. Rather, we may feel that it is God living His life through us, and therefore, everything—pleasure and pain, happiness and sadness—comes from the one Source of all that is. God plays through us like a fine instrument, hitting any range of notes of His own choosing—for all is made from the musical streams of Ananda/Bliss.

Sri Yukteswarji, an incarnation of wisdom, is a flawless compass guiding us to the Eternal. Such wisdom can be very strict, crushing our meandering dreams and ruthlessly severing our attachments. This is all done without malice but with the greatest love and solicitude. In fact, all that this great God-man did was done to bring about a revelation that all creation is an explosion of Ananda-Bliss—and as such, the realization that we are part and parcel made up of sacred Joy.

---

29 (pp. 415–6).

You have both the wisdom of the wise in you, and you are a being of bliss without end. This is what Sri Yukteswarji came to awaken in Master, and in us all.

Editor's Note: In *The Second Coming of Christ*, Paramhansa Yogananda speaks to the nature of a disciple. Here is Master's rendition of what Jesus looked for in Nathanael/Bartholomew who became a disciple among the inner circle of the twelve apostles. These beautiful words serve to show how well Master understood how one develops "the wisdom of the wise:"

Prophecy does not mean that all happenings on earth, including earthly human affairs, are predestined. It is not an art that can be practiced reliably by those who possess some small degree of psychic power. All events that have happened in the past have vibratory impressions in the ether, which sensitive people may sometimes tune into as mental images or vision. Similarly, the karmic law of cause and effect projects into the ether vibratory potentials of future events that are probably outcome, or effect, of previously initiated causes. Future events forming in the ether from causes originated by human actions are not always inevitable; they evolve and can change dramatically according to the transmuting power of man's free-will actions integrating into those karmic vibrations. One who has the ability to link past and future may predict a certain outcome according to extant conditions; but if those conditions are altered, the outcome may negate the foretelling. Doomsday "prophets" find themselves embarrassingly duped by their imagination and misreading of heavenly and scriptural signs.

Only the rare true prophet who is in tune with the will of God can make sure and accurate predictions, such as the foreseeing of the coming of Jesus. Such God-given predictions are concerned little with temporal matters that blow in the winds of whimsical human actions and their effects. Their primary and loftier purpose is to influence the spiritual betterment of man with both encouraging and cautionary revelations.

Thus, Moses and Isaiah and the prophets of the Old Testament who foretold the advent of Jesus were able by intuitive foresight, to trace the law of cause and effect which governs the drama of human existence. They knew also the law of God that sends self-emancipated, Christlike souls onto the earth at different ages, when the masses, burdened with the sin of ignorance, are in dire need of the light.

[Jesus in seeking disciples sought to] Behold a soul that is free from satanic insincerity . . . Guileless means sincerity, the simplicity or natural state of one's true being, free from duplicity, dissembling, hypocrisy, and all other serf-serving guises. It has no association with crudeness or rude hurtfulness in the name of being honest. The quiet humility of guilelessness is the sapience that distinguishes a truly spiritual personality. What magnetism it has! Sincerity is a virtue of virtues in the realm of spirituality. All other qualities a disciple may offer as the sum of his being at the feet of the guru must borrow a great measure of their worth from sincerity. Words and deeds are a sham without it. But a heart that is pure in its intention is the way to touch the heart of God.[30]

---

30   (pp. 197–8).

March 14

SPIRITUAL REBOOT

The enlightened brain's operating system.**

As many of us know, if a computer or one of our electronic gadgets is slowing down or stalling, the easiest, and oftentimes most effective, way to get things working is to turn the darn thing off, and then start it again; it's called a reboot. Computer problems can stem from software stuck in a loop it can't get out of, or if the hardware interface is malfunctioning—so, restart the computer and voila, more times than not, it fixes the problem!

The "software of your mind" can also get stuck in a continuous loop. Thinking, thinking, thinking, always thinking on some topic, some obsession, some object of desire or fear, or simply an endless loop of a commercial jingle you heard (if you have ever been on Disneyland's ride "It's a Small World," then you will have been subjected to this kind of diabolical jingle/abuse programming)! Anytime such a tune gets going in my head, I sing Ram Nam to the tune to be deprogrammed. It almost always breaks the cyclic nature of the tune, and even if it doesn't, I am still continuously singing the Name of God.

The body's hardware can also get stuck in repeating cycles: tense muscles in the neck, jaw, eyes, or back—well, anywhere you have muscles, they can become tense and remain that way. Your blood pressure gets higher, digestive secretions secrete way too much—there are so many ways for the body-hardware to malfunction, resulting in power drains, bloatware clogging, and inflammation of the operating system, even leading to catastrophic body failures.

A realignment of the body, mind, and Spirit can reboot your system, making for maximal function. One of the simplest ways of doing this is in our bi-daily meditation. We may begin our meditation with our thinking-software wasting mental computing power by looping certain thoughts, and our body-hardware tense and out of sorts. Now, if we spend our entire meditation time simply stuck in these loops, or thinking about what is going wrong in our body or our life, that is not meditation at all, and it will definitely not reboot our system.

To properly reboot our body and mind, this must be turned off—we must have a significant shift during meditation. In Kriya, our life-force moves in a circuit through our spine and brain; in Hong-Sau and Ram Nam, our mind is focused on the mantra. The result: our breathing is significantly slowed, we feel a release of tension from our body, and we enter into a quiet zone that not only slows our breathing, but our thinking transforms into pure witness awareness—we become the observer of all that is. A deeper breath, an even bigger release of tension, and we enjoy surpassingly beautiful peace; the joy of Spirit bubbles up from a deep Source in us and we feel expansive—our system is now being rebooted.

Sometimes a computer problem can be solved with a quick restart. In meditation terms, we take a few minutes during the day to reset our body-mind-Spirit system. Other times, the computer needs a whole system shut down; we then wait for some time for a cold restart—meditation-wise, this means going deeper and soaring higher until we have the solution and freedom we are looking for. Reverend Jill is taking some months in silence now—when God gives us the opportunity and the prompting, this can be a wonderfully deep reboot for our entire system.

It is not that simply spending more time in meditation results in progress, but that there is something about extended meditations being required for going deeper. With increased time, internal operating flaws are met, and a newly downloaded code allows for higher planes of consciousness. It may not always be the fact that something "incredible" occurs; rather, it may be a grounded, deepened awareness in Spirit that is being established. During my year of silence and solitude, an inner stillness was established in my heart-center that has stayed with me continuously, no matter the outer circumstances. Of course, with stillness, there is no fear—there is only perfect trust and reliance upon God alone.

Now, to a computer engineer, the circuitry of a motherboard may look beautiful. However, that does not compare in the least to the beauty of the lotus-brain streaming with Light: a manifestation of the Divine Motherboard. And with inner-vision, we can also see the life-force flowing throughout the subtle body system. What elegance of design, with speeds surpassing that of electrons or even light—complete downloads at the rate of perfectly synced thought-transference.

So, whether it is a shorter meditational restart or a deeper complete shutdown, let us look for the signs that make us know we have had a successful reboot. Then we will maximize our body-mind workstation and wonderfully synchronize with God's Mainframe of Divine Consciousness.

March 17

YOU ARE THE FULFILLMENT OF THE SACRED SCRIPTURES

Vulture Peak, Arizona, with teddy bear cactus
in the foreground: Amazing desert life, flowing.

Being active is a consequence of being in a physical body: our heart pumps, thoughts flow, muscles move; everywhere we look, creation is an expression of life-energy. Here in the desert, there is a surprising amount of life. There are remarkable varieties of cacti, odd-looking kangaroo rats with long back legs, and magnificent vultures flying over the peak named after them; these names may not seem appealing, but they are all quite interesting and amazing to see. One note of caution, though, there is a variety of teddy bear cactus that may seem like something soft that you could hold like a teddy bear; however, do not be deceived; these cacti have vicious spines and host painful microscopic barbs that don't like to let go, once attached!

Throughout all of this magnificent desert, vital life-force flows and animates all we see. Mountains, plants, and birds are all vibrant, and live mostly by nature's design, leaving little room for independence. When we get into the higher forms of mammals, we see more examples of will and independence, but only with the human being do we see a real development of abstract thought, self-reflection, and an independence of will that can either go seriously astray from its original design, or else, be mastered and transformed into transcendent Consciousness. Sinners and saints are almost exclusively the province of the human species.

During this cycle in the planet's evolution, there are times when we have seen more of the sinner than the saint. Nevertheless, the innate capacity for divinity is ever present in one and all. Some of the most magnificent scriptures ever penned come from St. John and bear this inherent potential: "In the beginning was the Word, and the Word was with God, and the Word was God. The same was true in the beginning with God. All things were made by him, and without him was not anything made that was made. In him was life; and the life was the light of men. And the light shineth in darkness; and the darkness comprehended it not" (John 1:1–5).

The Light shines in the Darkness.

The mystery is how the Light can shine in the darkness and yet it is not seen. The Vedas explain the inexplicable by means of maya: a veil of delusion that makes creation ignorant of its own Divinity. Maya does not alter the Eternal Substance that is God, but it is a sleight of hand that makes the darkness of creation incapable of comprehending the ever-present Light.

However, there is a built-in failsafe: the Savior is the Light seeded in humanity and is present in everything that is made. So, the thing is to discover that Reality—to accept deeply into our being the light of truth that has always been with us. No individual could ever match the description of this universal Savior. The notion that Jesus is the exclusive expression of that Light flies in the face of the fact that that Light is in every person walking the earth. The Light was awakened in our dear savior Jesus, even as it can become awakened in each and every one of us.

This is the good news of the gospel. It is more than good news, but superlatives seem not to touch the essence of this great revelation—God within us and God born in man. God is a Reality that we may know in truth through direct inner experience. In fact, we are all made up of God-stuff; this remarkable news has yet to be known by an unsuspecting humanity. Emmanuel—God with us—is really that, God with us in every human being!

It is our inborn Light of Dharma that demands that we awaken to this greater Reality. We close our eyes, go within, and discover the sacred life-force flowing throughout our being; then our divine awareness can expand out to the furthest reaches of space. With the inner sight awakened, we open our two eyes and comprehend the same sacred force operating through all of nature, in all of humanity, in every living thing in space. We have awakened to Christ Consciousness, we have ascended, and in seeing this, we know the Heavenly Father—we realize, "I am That."

Surely, we see that, do we not? Surely God is awakening this Reality in us—how can He not? I only write what He writes through this form. His word cannot be stillborn but must live and find fulfillment. This is the reason we are here. Destiny must be fulfilled in us. Having realized this eternal Truth—when we act, we serve. For we only live to serve the One who is in all. Our heart pumps, thoughts flow, muscles move, and it is all an expression of the Light in us that is in service to the Light in all.

We are the fulfillment of the sacred scriptures.

Beautiful Spirit shines throughout Nature.

March 21

FIERCE GRACE

Yogacharya David on a hike near
Vulture Peak, Arizona, March 18, 2019.

Dear All,

This will be a different kind of discourse. On Monday, Carla and I were out for a hike near Vulture Peak. I was feeling very strong, flying up the hills without strain. On Tuesday, we had gone to do errands in Surprise, Arizona, and while walking, I felt my knees getting weak. When we returned to the motorhome where we were camping, my legs were not very strong; in fact, my knees felt like jelly. I tried to make it up the steps, but the portable step collapsed, and I went down.

When I got into the motorhome, I was not able to sit up straight, nor did I have any strength in my left side. I realized something had happened and that we needed to go to the hospital. When we arrived at the hospital, Carla told them I was having a stroke and they came rushing out. They took me in for a CT scan. They found blood in my frontal lobe. The blood was caused by a mass irritating the brain cells, which was causing the stroke. This is called a hemorrhagic stroke, different from what we usually think of when someone is having a stroke.

Even though I was in this state, my speech was all right and my sense of humor intact. There was a sign on the wall that said, "If you assault a caregiver, it is a felony." If Carla wanted something, the nurse had suggested just yelling for them. I pointed at the sign, and I said, "I read the sign." She looked a little startled and then broke out in gales of laughter!

Later, she said, "I told everyone what you said. Everyone loves coming into this room and that's unusual for someone in your situation. You are so calm; there is something very special about you." She kept on repeating this over and over. She also said "You look so young! You have found the secret to the Fountain of Youth!"

My condition was more than this community hospital could handle and the doctor was dithering. I needed Magnetic Resonance Imaging (MRI)[31] and wanted to go back to the Northwest to my saintly doctor, Dr. S., so our "angel" nurse went in and told the doctor what she needed to do.

I was flown by helicopter to St. Joseph's Hospital in Phoenix. The view of the city lights was magnificent as we came in. I was taken to the Intensive Care Unit (ICU) and have been given

---

31   Magnetic Resonance Imaging (MRI) scanners use strong magnetic fields to view the body organs.

computerized tomography CT/MRI scans and a variety of tests.[32] This is a teaching hospital and is well known for its neurology department, which provides the exact kind of care that I need. God's Grace. The doctor was in this morning and said that with this type of stroke, the initial symptoms are more severe, but the long-term progress is better. Right now, I have no strength in my left arm and limited mobility in my left leg, so by necessity, we will be down here for the next few months.

This has all been quite a shock since I was feeling so perfectly well beforehand. Right now, the doctors do not know where this came from. It is a mystery to them. The doctor had been worried because the blood flow in the brain had been expanding; as of this morning, it is not.

We will be here for some months for rehabilitation. Jerry and Lois were here yesterday with us and are a great support. Larry will fly down on Friday. Obviously, this is going to change some of our future plans. I'm sorry to say we will not be up for Easter, nor is it likely we will be at Loon Lake.

Throughout this time, I have felt such a closeness to Swami Satchidananda and know all he went through due to a stroke. I'm dictating this posting to Carla as typing is difficult. I've also felt close to Mother. I know that she went through so much. I remember the time she was giving a talk and she had a stroke. Normally, I had my eyes closed as I sat behind her, yet for some reason, I opened my eyes and saw her weaving back and forth. Somehow, God arranged it for me to get up and catch her before she fell. I immediately took her to Billie's car, and she drove her to Northwest Hospital.

The idea for entitling this post *Fierce Grace* came from Richard Alpert, known as Ram Dass, (disciple of the great Neem Karoli

---

32   Computerized tomography (CT) scans take X-ray images from different angles around the body.

Baba) who made a documentary about his experience of having a stroke.

I'm sorry to have to deliver this difficult news. I know it's not what you want to hear, nor is it what I want to write. Who can doubt that I am following in the footsteps of some of the greatest souls I have had the pleasure to know? Fierce Grace, INDEED!

March 31

REHABILITATION: WEEK 2

St. Francis Statue in the Peace Garden at
St. Joseph's Medical Center, Phoenix, Arizona.

Dear Beloved in God,

God has lined up quite a time for me. Just in case you didn't think a hemorrhagic stroke was enough, He decided to give me gastrointestinal problems, and I became extremely dehydrated. I could not eat, which has affected my energy level and ability to think clearly. All of that is on the mend now.

All of these challenges have drawn my mind back to God, more urgently relying upon His strength, submitting to His will in this, as in all, things.

Thank you for your prayers, cards, emails, and to all those who have supported me at this time. Carla stands foremost in that legion, along with Jerry and Lois, and Rick and Judy who have been a great support to Carla who is trying to manage so many things at once.

In 1933, Master wrote a meditation for March 31st:

> I will contact God constantly through the peace of all hearts. I will behold Him on the Altar of My Silence. I will merge in the Eternal One through the Bliss of Meditation.
> —PARAMHANSA YOGANANDA

It is through His Omniscience that I feel you living your lives, taking sure and courageous steps towards God-realization. Surely, we are all in His hands each and every moment of the day.

The consequence of what God has given me has made me focus on one day at a time, one moment at a time, one victory at a time. That is all that we have or will ever have when we focus on Him—we feel time and space spread out into all eternity. I have a body, but I am not this body: I have a mind, but I am not this mind. I remain in the Eternal Spirit of God: the one sole Reality.

There is a lovely Peace Garden here at the hospital that Carla has taken me to, where there is a statue of St. Francis surrounded by living flowers and birdsong. To think about St. Francis, Mother, and Swamiji, and about all the difficulties they went through, provides me with great strength. It is in the secret blessing of suffering that there is a radiance that goes from that one when he or she is attuned to God: this focus helps lift the world's burdens.

Know that I hold you in my heart, and that in God there is no separation in time or space—only oneness, only union in God.

April 4

GET YOUR MIRACLE!

Christine Baldigara: "Get Your Miracle!" Maple Ridge, B.C., 2009.

Beloved Children of the Infinite, God gave me a very interesting experience the other night. I woke up around 1:30 a.m. in terrific pain—it felt like a nail being driven into the nerve behind my knee. These pains have been coming on my left side as a sign of nerves awakening from the paralysis; however, this felt more intense and difficult. Normally, when such pains come to me in the night, I consider it a good sign. I have used distilled oil of comfrey that was a gift from Zach and Hailey, and in most cases, the pain then goes away. However, in this powerful experience, the pain remained intense—God thought to reveal a great truth in this manner. He guided my thoughts toward the question, "Why is there cruelty in the world?"

So, I asked God, "In creating this universe, why did You allow cruelty to be part of it when it is nothing but a joyful expression of Yourself?" And what He told me, "For every such thing, it awakens its opposite." For cruelty awakens divine compassion, not always in a moment or a day, and as divine compassion spreads over this world, cruelty will be canceled out. If humanity had not erred by going against God's harmony in the first place, there would be no such need for a counterbalancing law.

So, when we see discord and inharmony in this world, even cruelty, let them awaken compassionate love in us; we can then be even more determined to be a bearer of Light and Love. As each of us does this, we will build a collective strength that one day will result in cruelty being something only known in history books. Until that day comes, we are called upon to be warriors of compassion. Such wisdom came from God during this experience that—words—can never fully convey.

Rehabilitation Continued: I want to thank you for all your prayers, cards, and emails. Last week was a very rough one as gastrointestinal problems and dehydration affected my energy and concentration. As of today, I can tell you I feel more fully myself once again—renewed energy, renewed concentration, and all of my rehabilitation test scores have vastly improved this week. Carla had the idea to start a "Miracle List" each night, noting the improvements we have noticed throughout the day. Years ago, when people came for time with me while I was in Maple Ridge, Christine would always say, "Get your miracle," in a lyrical voice. I think of that now when we make our "Miracle List" at the end of the day—a list of firsts. Every night, we have had ten or twelve things of note. Today, I was able to open and close my left hand smoothly and evenly whereas before it had been a struggle. This early morning, I was doing multiplication tables mentally that were difficult for me last week. I am now solving story problems that require inferences and concentration that sent me into a tizzy the day before. My sense of balance for sitting and standing continues to grow. So, what I would like to suggest to you is that you pay attention to the little and big miracles in your life—"Get your miracle!"

April 7

A GOD-CENTERED LIFE

Yogacharya David: With Loving Pronams, 2019.

With Loving Pronams

The value of living a life centered in God is never so evident as when we face life's greatest challenges. For that is the time when having the strength that God-awareness brings with it is required: knowing His never-failing goodness, accepting His love, and bowing to the peace that comes with perfect resignation to His will.

The human way is to question why a seemingly untoward thing is happening. Fear and anger can run rampant with a consequent feeling of being cut off from God, the Source of all virtue and right action.

God does not pull the rug out from underneath us, so to speak, simply to vex us, nor is it a mechanistic universe that does all without thought or caring. If our eye of intuition is opened to the universal vision, and we see a glowing intelligence behind all life, and we see demonstrated before us His Grace operating in and around us, then we can undergo a marvelous transformation in which we know that we are never alone, never without direction, and never without the strength to meet life's challenges.

So, let us cheerfully meet the world and know God as our sole (Soul) support, comforter, and guide.

Miracle List Update: Today, I am typing this using my left hand. This morning, I lifted my left hand to my left shoulder. My left leg has shown signs of voluntary movement. My left-side peripheral vision has vastly improved and sustained concentration is much stronger—these were all affected by the hemorrhage on the right side of my brain There are too many improvements to list here. This morning, for the first time, I can move my left leg and actually feel some strength there. I continue in rehabilitation boot camp here, where they ask the impossible so that they might get the possible. Rick and Judy are leaving for the "great white north," as they have maxed out their allowed time for being out of the country. They have both been a God-send and done yeoman's seva along with Jerry and Lois who will remain here. And, of course, Carla, who, after driving here while chasing the helicopter to the ICU, has not left my side, at one point even sleeping on the floor; all the while, she has been making my life a million, million times easier—she has been a rock. And to you, dear ones, prayer warriors for Team Total Recovery, with too many assists to count—my deepest love and gratitude. Victory to God, Victory to the Light!

April 14

LIMITATIONS ARE A STARTING POINT

Yogacharya David doing physical
therapy in the rehabilitation gym.

I t has been wonderful to see this body gradually waking up to its
normal functions. Usually, we identify with the body and gauge
how we are doing based on that. Our other point of reference
is the mind—am I thinking clearly? Can I solve problems? When
God took me through the three mystical crucifixions, He made
it perfectly clear that I have a body, but I am not this body, and I
have a mind, but I am not the mind—the Source of my existence
is the eternal Spirit residing within and without.

That knowledge has allowed me to focus on healing this body
and not spend time in doubt and worry. It also helps me to live

in the moment and not in the future of "What ifs," or a past of "What was," but to remain in the here and now.

We had a speaker come to a family support group with a remarkable story. Seven years ago, she had a stroke and was in a coma for two and a half months. When she woke up, she was blind, had a poor memory, and could not walk. She was in therapy for 18 months and could not be at home on her own for two and a half years. Today, she walked into our meeting and you would not suspect anything unusual about her. She spoke eloquently about her experiences. She continues to work to compensate for memory lapses, writes notes to herself, and continues to use her shampoo trick even though she does not need it anymore—in the past, she could not remember if she had washed her hair or not, so she pushed the shampoo bottle forward if she had washed her hair and then placed it on the back of the shelf if she had not.

A main point she made was that when the doctor told her she would be in a wheelchair for six more months, she took it as a challenge to get out faster: she was out of her chair in three months. When her daughter-in-law said she could not hold her grandchild until she could prove she could do it safely, she went to work strengthening herself until she could. Now she regularly babysits her grandchildren. I thought, "What a wonderful example for living life! To take challenges not as limitations, but as starting points." When told that you cannot do a certain thing, take it as a challenge to prove that you can. Such a commitment spurs you to build yourself up. No need to be held back by artificial constraints. Another main point she made—do not define yourself by your body or its limitations; who you are is not your body or mind. Today, seven years later, she continues to set goals for progress even though she is no longer in therapy.

We all have obstacles of one kind or another; some of them are obvious to others and some blend into the background—away from public view.

One time, Mother was riding in a car with a devotee. There were no parking spots except in the one marked for the disabled. Mother said, "You can park there." The devotee pointed out that it was for disabled people. Mother said, "That's all right; in the body, we are all disabled!" They parked and did not get a ticket. Being with the guru is always an eye-opening experience!

Therapy Update: I am kept busy here with five or six hours of various types of therapies on weekdays for the body and mind (two hours a day on the weekends). Recent progress shows increased cognitive function, that my stamina has steadily grown, the beginning of the activation in my left hip, leg, and foot has begun (first comes the activation of the muscles, then strengthening the response, and then the muscles grow stronger); also, standing and sitting (with assistance) are smoother and with better balance. I slept through the night for the first time on Friday night. Periodic nerve pain in my left leg has reduced and I am also dressing myself with greater self-reliance. Everything I can do for myself, I do—when we put the demand on the brain, it responds by clearing old pathways or creating new ones. The muscles are intact; what is needed is the brain's connection to the body.

With Loving Pronams

Thank you for all the lovely cards, emails, and texts, and of course, your prayers; all are lovingly received. The staff here have all commented on the rapid recovery they are seeing in this body. This recovery is, in no small measure, a result of your positive thoughts and prayers. Please receive my loving pronams in return.

April 21

MAY CHRIST BE RISEN IN YOU TODAY

Jesus ascending into the heavenly Light.

"May Christ be risen in you today."

This is an ancient orthodox Easter morning Christian greeting. John D. wrote this to me in an email. He sent those greetings on to me, and in turn, I send them on to you. I thought it such a beautiful blessing. This implicit message is that the Christ story is everyone's hidden potential—the Christ Principle is part and parcel of the human being's makeup.

How remarkable when the life and teachings of Jesus the Christ jump off the pages from ancient texts and awaken a sleeping God-hood within. Mother Hamilton did that for me—she made the Christ live in me and showed me the way to realize our one Father-God. The power of God in her helped awaken the sleeping God in me, and for that, she has my eternal gratitude.

Mother took me on such a tremendous journey, physically demanding, mentally exacting, emotionally expanding—in short, it tested me in every possible way and in more ways than I could have ever anticipated. From the Mystical Crucifixion of the physical, energetic, and mental, each stage carried its own tests and upliftment. Surely, there is no greater challenge and no comparable reward.

Jesus came in a line of perfect incarnations that our Heavenly Father has sent to show us the way back to him. We error when we make a god of one of his incarnations and neglect the primary message that the same God that is in him is in us. To clarify that message: God and the Kingdom of Heaven are to be found within us.

Let us prove to ourselves the truth of these teachings on this Easter Day, and every day, by going within and realizing that the great Reality is waiting to resurrect itself in us. Words do not do it; reading will not get us there. Only by knowing that the Kingdom of Heaven is within will we come face to face with the living Christ.

April 26

HOMECOMING

Mother Hamilton: A picture of
indomitable will, Seattle, early 1970s.

t is a little over a month since I started intensive rehabilitation. Time to go home. We got on a plane and flew back to
the Northwest, back to Camano Island. Jerry drove us to the
airport. Wheelchair transportation was arranged in advance from
the curb to the plane seat. The entire flight went as smoothly as
we could hope.

Before leaving the hospital, I met with Dr. K., the "physical doctor" who has monitored my progress during rehabilitation. She
said, "We don't want to see you go; you have been our 'super-
star.'" My physical, occupational, and speech therapists echoed
the same sentiments. Earlier, when I said, "I will lift my foot to

the wheelchair foot-support," something I had not yet managed, my occupational therapist said, "I have no doubt that in a couple of days, you will. I have never seen anyone like you. You say you will do something, and two days later, you do it. You have such a strong will." I feel these comments are reflections on my guru who demonstrated such a strong will and set the pattern for me to emulate.

It has been interesting being out of the hospital after such a lengthy stay—being in traffic, and the activity at the airport—all this gave a shock to my healing brain. Even though everything went smoothly, I found I could not move my left leg by the end of the flight; in fact, the last hour of the flight was excruciating. I played Papa's Ram Nam on my phone, and he made it possible to endure it.

In the contained environment of the rehabilitation center, my brain had made new connections and advanced; out in the world, my brain struggled to absorb it all. I was also fighting off the first signs of a cold. Many of the advancements I had made have been temporarily lost. Yesterday, I slept through much of the day. Today, I am making slow progress toward being back to myself, noticing windows of time when I have greater control over my body movements, less pain, and clearer thinking. I am also overcoming the cold—it never got a grip on me. This trip has had a greater shock to my system than I anticipated.

The other factor I find interesting is that while in rehabilitation, inner experiences ebbed, allowing for full concentration on healing the body. As soon as I came into the house, I heard and felt the powerful Aum and I entered into an interior state of being. God's Presence is manifest in the rehabilitation center and in the house, both in their unique ways; however, a definite shift to interior consciousness has come since arriving home. This is God's inscrutable play, and He is in charge of it all, and He works for the highest good in all He does.

I arrived home to a bountiful display of nature's colors—so many vases full of flowers. There was also a refrigerator/freezer full of food made with such love, and modifications for the house—a ramp and handrails, thanks to Greg and Jill, a yard looking perfect, thanks to Rebecca, get-well cards and loving acts of service by so many helping, loving hands, all done in seva to God—my heart overflows with gratitude. We will continue to monitor how the brain heals and recovers from the stroke and the trip home. Right now, this brain and body need to rest in Him and be surcharged with His sacred life-force.

April 28

THE BENEFITS OF A SPIRITUAL LIFE

The lilies of the field.**

People leading a materialistic life can find happiness, and lead a moral and ennobling life—so why bother to have a spiritual discipline? For many of us, there is simply no other choice that satisfies our inner need for Divine union. Also, there are many practical reasons that only a spiritual life can satisfy. True spiritual experience brings unsurpassed peace, inner assurance, expanding bliss, a knowledge of who and what we truly are, and an intuitive understanding and realization that only comes with upliftment in consciousness. Truly, there is no greater life that can be had.

It is definitely not the easiest journey to take; there are no other journeys that challenge us to the core to the same degree; also, there will not be any that can lift us so high. Once we have had an experience in transcendent consciousness, we will feel that before, we were sleepwalking in life. It is as if the scales fall from our eyes, and we see inner and outer reality in a brand-new way. There are many who appreciate the beauty of a flower but with what eyes of realization did Jesus see these flowers when he made the statement:

"Consider the lilies of the field, how they grow; they toil not, neither do they spin: And yet I say unto you, that even Solomon in all his glory was not arrayed like one of these" (Matthew 6: 28–29).

Once, I was walking through the woods when I was suddenly lifted into the Causal plane. The rocks, trees, and path were the same, but I saw them as expressions of subtle, beautiful ideas; my own body was also made up of the same Causal realm, a realm far more beautiful and of greater dimensions than the Astral realm. I understood that before material expression, everything exists as an idea of the Creator. That idea-form is far more than imagination and has a reality much greater than this material form. It seems impossible to convey in words this majestic, super-natural realm.

Oftentimes, we can think the Astral and Causal Realms are distant places, far removed from this material plane. However, spiritual experiences have taught me that these realities are all around—the substrata of all we see in the material world. We truly live in a magnificent creation, and we only scratch the surface of what is all around us.

I sit here, surrounded in Aum vibration, resounding within and without; life-force twinkles in walls, floor, and in every material thing; the Divine Presence is blissfully thick in the air; only a spiritual awakening can open the doors to such realities. This is not my province only, but the inborn nature of us all. Let us not live on the surface of life; let us dive deep into the Reality that Divine union alone can bring us.

Health Update: Spiritual perception is not dependent upon a perfect body. This body suffered a temporary setback after the trip back to the northwest. I am gradually recovering from that, gaining use and strength in my left leg; my left arm fared better and I continue to touch-type all of these discourses (I have typed all but the first discourse after my stroke), and some of my mental executive functions have been affected and are gradually returning.

This explanation comes from our in-house medical expert on returning home and the challenges and opportunities this brings. Ruth writes to Carla:

1. We spoke of on-days and recuperation-days; on-days that include a rehabilitation schedule and recuperation-days that are absolutely off. No subconscious guilt here. This is important, as the push David has been under, rightly so, with rehabilitation experts, was possibly too much for his sympathetic nervous system at the time, but necessary. Now he needs rest and recuperation time, so, maybe for a few weeks more recuperation days. He will know as will you. This is being kind to the parasympathetic nervous system. It most likely has been stretched and needs recalibration to a better norm. It is the "repair and heal" system.

   When the Autonomic Nervous system (sympathetic nervous system and parasympathetic nervous system) balances, the primitive brain will downgrade alert. Then, there will be more natural energy for progress versus mind-based mental push energy needed up until now. But in the long run, this "push" can bring exhaustion.

2. The world outside the hospital is different, as David noted. A very different environment. So, now, bring a sensible and patient and balanced rehabilitation to the home. It must be different as it is two different worlds. Plus, the body needs to integrate. This can bring a "twosteps forward, one step back" experience. This is normal. Honor the cells. With each shift, 1000s of cells must change, and there are 100s of 1000s of nervous system decoding DNA messages and gene changes. A stressed and tired body does not always send information in the correct order, or it can take detours. Persistence, of course, with mountains of Hope and sincere Intention, always wins to the maximum. However, please let wise patience be your friend.

Mountains of hope/faith and sincere intention are absolutely intact, along with your healing thoughts and prayers. Failure is not an option for Team Total Recovery. Thanks for being on the team. Jai Gurus!

May 1

SPIRITUAL YOGA AND REHABILITATION

St. Francis, a Yogi-Christ for the ages.

Yoga, as we know, is far more than a system of physical exercises; it is a complete set of methods that seek to guide us toward ideal physical, mental, and spiritual health. Through Kriya Yoga, we are given the highest teachings to attain awakened spiritual enlightenment because we develop the higher centers of consciousness in the spine and the brain. Yoga is a practical philosophy with measurable goals to be attained in physical health and enlightenment.

Applying these methods during my time in rehabilitation has made it possible for me to make progress, which has astonished the various therapists working with me. Here are some of the methods and results:

Meditation: Of course, meditation is at the core of our spiritual practice. While there are many benefits to this practice, its ultimate goal: helping us become established in the Self has been of enormous value. The Self remains unmoved in a world of constant change. This un-movability keeps the changeable/reactive self-rooted in the immutable core of our Being. As a result, there is no wasted energy transferred into fear and uncertainty. Rather, the mind is focused on what needs to happen now—this is of great benefit in rehabilitation because a total mind-focus is needed for even the simplest of actions.

Faith and Devotion: A feeling of love and devotion for God gives one a sense of connectedness and removes the feeling of isolation that can come with circumstances in which one has a lack of control. Feeling that God and Gurus are with us each step of the way brings strength and a knowledge that all is going according to the Divine Plan. The hand of God is ever with us in the most loving way. When pain comes, it is turned over to God, and we are given the ability to endure it or rise above it. Our best Friend is always with us, and this is a wonderful comfort.

Gratitude: When we have a long history of being conscious of things that make us grateful to our Creator, we are aware of more than the challenges we face. We see unnumbered things to be grateful for. This is no small thing when healing from an injury.

Energization Exercises: Master gave us a gift through his Energization Exercises. As I lay in bed in the early morning hours, I practice tensing and releasing and feeling the life-force flowing into body parts. Even those parts in my leg and arm that did not respond to physical tensing, I have no doubt, were being awakened by the mental focus of guiding energy to those muscle groups. As they woke up, the tensing started with minute movements; now it has grown stronger and is done with more control.

Alternate Nostril Breathing: Erin lovingly sent me information on the benefits of alternate nostril breathing. Practitioners have done studies for stroke patients in rehabilitation. This type of breathing has been proven to speed up recovery time. Early morning hours have been set aside for this practice, as well as sporadic times during the day. This practice has a calming effect along with improved focus for the mind.

Discernment: With Spiritual attunement comes discernment for what is true. On different occasions, nurses gave me their own ideas as facts that were untrue. On the first occasion, the nurse said in conversation that, of course, I had a stroke, as I was older. Just like a car wears out and needs a new transmission, or other repairs, we will get sick and wear out with age, then she walked out of the room. Later, when she returned, I said that I had thought about what she said. I said, "Our bodies are different than machines. A car cannot repair itself, and even in this moment, my body is doing just that in a miraculous way. Our bodies are working miracles and right nutrition, right thinking, and God can heal what ails the body." She agreed, and in a short time, she changed from someone who looked to be carrying the world on her shoulders to smiling, laughing, and she took wonderful care of me—in the end, as I was leaving, she gave me a big hug and said how sorry she was that I was leaving.

In another case, a nurse who had taken good care of me said it was only a matter of time before I had another stroke. I said, "I don't agree. I will follow the doctor's instructions," which was what she wanted to scare me into. "I understand there are statistics, but I am not a statistic: God's will reigns supreme, and if He wills it, I will recover my full health."

Such messages received by a weakened mind can be receptive soil and give birth to self-fulfilling prophesies. I utterly rejected them then, and I still do. We must be careful that our thoughts and words comport with the highest truth and promote the greatest good.

Prana Life-Force: Life-force, or Prana, is the underlying cause of healing as it works through the cells and our intelligence. It also gives us the power of movement. Many times a day, I focus my mind at the back of my head and along my spine, to move this body when I am standing, walking, and moving my arm; I feel the difference.

Clearing/Charging Breath: Many of you who have taken the class will know the Clearing/Charging Breath which I have freely employed throughout my rehabilitation time. This breathing practice has proven to be extremely useful for pain relief. I plan to use more of the Charging Breath going into the future for strengthening different body parts.[33]

Chanting: Chanting is unparalleled for keeping the mind on God and feeling His Bliss.

Spiritual Family and Kindred Spirits: The great good that has come from this time is being able to appreciate the love and support that I have received from our spiritual family and kindred spirits around the world. I have felt the power of prayer, received cards, and emails that reflect the Godhood in devotees in ways I have not seen manifest before. I do believe there is a swell of

---

33   For a full outline of the "Clearing and Charging Breath Practice," see the Appendix of *Silence: Entering the Cosmic Sea of Consciousness.*

spiritual consciousness that is lifting us higher, and for that, I have tremendous gratitude.

Gratitude For All That I Have Been Given: The value of these yoga methods cannot be overstated. I am filled with gratitude for God and Gurus and His Saints through whom His Grace flows. Every day, Carla and I visited St. Francis' statue in the Healing Garden; at the hospital, we pronamed to him and asked his blessing for all the patients in the hospital and for all the caregivers as well. What Grace has poured on this head and blessed me in untold ways!

May 5

DO WORKS IN HOLINESS

Arjuna's call to battle: *Krishna Tells the Gita to Arjuna.***

For the past forty-five years, I have had a constant companion, a little book with a poetic rendition of the *Bhagavad Gita*, printed in 1904; it is the same translation that Master and Papa carried with them (by Sir Edwin Arnold). It has been a source of inspiration and insight that has remained fresh and alive through the years. Some others have told me its poetic translation makes it difficult to penetrate, but I have always found it a reflection of the Gita's Sanskrit that makes it a "Song Celestial."

In the fifth chapter of the Gita, Arjuna wants clarification from Krishna. At one point, Krishna has said to sit in meditation and go beyond creation as a focus for sadhana; yet, at other times, Krishna says to be active in the world and perform actions without attachment to the results—selfless service. Should we renounce the world and sit in meditation only, or fulfill our duty with the right attitude?

Arjuna:

> Yet, Krishna! at the one time thou dost laud
>   Surcease of works, and, at another time,
>   Service through work. Of these twain plainly tell
>   Which is the better way?

Krishna:

> To cease from works
>   Is well, and to do works in holiness
>   Is well; and both conduct to bliss supreme;
>   But of these twain the better way is his
>   Who working piously refraineth not.
>   That is the true Renouncer, firm and fixed,
>   Who—seeking nought, rejecting nought—dwells proof
>   Against the "opposites." O valiant Prince!
>   In doing, such breaks lightly from all deed:
>   'Tis the new scholar talks as they were two,
>   This Sankhya and this (Karma) Yoga: wise men know
>   Who husbands one plucks golden fruit of both!
>   . . . Whoso is fixed in holiness, self-ruled,
>   Pure-hearted, lord of senses and of self,
>   Lost in the common life of all which lives—
>   A "Yogayukt"—he is a Saint who wends

Straightway to Brahm. Such an one is not touched
By taint of deeds. "Nought of myself I do!"
Thus will he think—who holds the truth of truths.[34]

There are few who can retire from the activities of life full-time and exclusively merge into God. Better to lead a life of balance, fulfill your duties in life, and purify your body and mind by being "in the world, not of the world." Time in meditation anchors us to the true Self—then we can go out into this world and do all as His faithful servant. With such a right attitude, we merge and become one with highest consciousness, seeing God as the sole doer.

---

34   Arnold, Edwin, Sir. (1904). *The Song Celestial; or Bhagavad Gita* (pp.55–56).

May 9

WILL POWER

Mother Hamilton: Personification of Will,
both human and Divine, Victoria, B.C., 1977.

W ill Power is a fundamental part of our individuality. It can be used for noble, constructive purposes, or it can equally be used to degrade life and be so weakened that we feel that we have lost ourselves. Even when we feel helpless in life against bad habits that work against us, we are actually using great amounts of will power—only in the negative.

Take someone, for instance, who has a drug addiction; that one may feel helplessly caught in the addiction; however, when it comes to feeding the habit, there is no end to the creativity and lengths that one will go to find the means for satisfying this crav-ing—that is an example of negative will power in action.

Tap into that same will power and train it to seek out good and positive ends, and what had seemed to be helplessness turns into empowerment. We can visualize our Self as the highest and best core part of us; it operates through our ego-self, and in turn, exercises will power throughout the mind and body. A spiritually tuned will is sensitively aligned to the Self or God's will. The Self always takes action for the highest good of everyone concerned and leads the soul to ultimate spiritual freedom.

The opposite of surrender to Divine Will is a mind driven by the dictates of the body or by people and surrounding circum-stances. The little self feels it does not have a choice in life when faced with the demands of the body and social pressure. Once again, when properly analyzed, great will power is being employed by the self to meet the cravings of the body and the expecta-tions from others, only it chooses to please others and sacrifice the self. You feel caught in a world of no choice; only, you will go to great lengths to do this, using a very strong will to do so. Let us take another example: you have a fear of heights, and you approach a cliff. Your reaction to falling will be swift with a pow-erful urge to avoid the edge of the cliff—a remarkable use of will in the moment.

Recognizing how powerful your will is—even when used for ends that do not serve you well—can be the beginning of "own-ing" your will. Then, it is a matter of going to the roots of your will power and learning to direct it to positive ends.

I have had great opportunities to do just that during my recov-ery. What before operated automatically through the left side of my body as muscle memory had to be learned all over again. The power to walk entails so much communication between the brain and the body—millions of calculations are going on throughout this process. It is something that we can take for granted when it is a well-worn pathway in the brain, nervous system, and muscular system. Take those pathways away, and now we are a toddler taking uncertain steps in a brand-new world.

Relearning to walk means every step is done mindfully and with great intention—the power of will used consciously. Fortunately, as an adult, I have awareness that transcends that of the toddler. I use the imaging power of my brain to mentally see myself taking steps smoothly, with strength and confidence, all the while remaining mindfully aware of staying safe. Mentally, I connect these actions coming from my core self, which in turn flows from my deeper Self—thus, even ordinary action becomes an expression of Divine Will. This inner attunement to spiritual grace greatly speeds up healing.

When I stand, I feel the movement of life-force flowing from behind me from an unlimited Source that enters the body through the back of my head and along my spine. This connection keeps me linked to the source of my strength, and, even when the body is exhausted from the effort, I keep that openness to the infinite supply of Spirit. I also affirm that I am made in the likeness and image of perfect Divine Consciousness; all things are possible and doable through Grace. Individual will, attuned to Divine Will, makes for our greatest advancement physically, mentally, and spiritually.

Health Update: My brain continues to heal. I am sometimes surprised at how everyday activities can tire the body and by the amount of rest they ask for afterward. Every day, there continue to be new "firsts." I take several trips a day, the length of the house, walking with the quad cane with Carla spotting me every step of the way, and I have even taken forays without using a cane at all. My left leg and arm continue to build strength and stamina—taking simple steps has never felt so good. Nerve pain caused by the brain sending signals through the wrong nerve pathways is slowly decreasing. So, there is much to be grateful for, and as always, you as members of Team Total Recovery, are at the top of my gratitude list.

May 12

THRICE BLESSED BY DIVINE MOTHER

Our Divine Mother: Mother
Hamilton, Seattle, c. 1976.

I have been thrice blessed—a recipient of extraordinary grace from the universal Divine Mother coming to me in human form. The first came as my physical mother who suffered through my birth into this world. As I was breech when still in the womb, she had tears that needed sutures afterward and then bed rest. After that, she gave me a lifetime of unconditional love made manifest through loving, caring acts; anything in her capacity to give, she gave to me. She always held out the best in me, even when I did not do so for myself.

I took a class while pursuing my degree in psychology—interpreting freehand family drawings. As students, we presented sketches we made of our family of origin, and the professor helped to bring out the deeper meaning of the drawings. I had pictured my mother sitting in a blue chair with a high back. The professor asked me questions about elements regarding the picture, then, he came to my mother and the chair. He said, "The blue back of the chair surrounds your mother's head is suggesting a halo. Do you think of your mother as a saint?" Knowing he had a Freudian point of view, I knew I was skating on thin ice. My courage rose to the occasion; I said, "Yes, I do." Surprisingly, he said, "That's good. I think of my mother in the same way." Whew!

For the ultimate spiritual journey, I was destined, and my mother could not help me. To give me a spiritual birth required someone with unique qualifications. Mother Hamilton had those qualifications, and more. The Divine Mother had descended to earth directly in her form to help devotees ascend to God-realization, and to help the world at large through a difficult transition toward higher spiritual consciousness. She lovingly called me to herself as I entered my twentieth year that I might take a second birth—a spiritual birth.

Mother Hamilton also saw the best in me when I did not always hold it for myself. She awakened divinity in me, taught me the truth, and was a perfect embodiment of being perfectly human and Divine. She also brought to me a remarkable guru-lineage and the spiritually perfected Swami (Papa) Ramdas. Each one of these supremely realized souls manifested pure divinity with a rich variety of expressions in their humanity. It helped me to know I need not be a carbon copy of any personality. Rather, I came to know that God delights in expressing Himself as unique, divine personalities.

Mother left the body before I had completed my full God-realization, so she guided me to the feet of Swami

Satchidananda—Papa's spiritual child. Interestingly, I came to think of Swamiji as my second spiritual mother. It was through the power of God in Mother and in Swamiji that I was lifted into the spiritual union that, for so many years, I had yearned. Through Swamiji's quiet ways, I was given yet another example of how God is uniquely expressed through a human personality. When Swamiji smiled, it was the Divine Mother who smiled through him.

From the beginning, I did not think of God as a personality. It has often been the case that devotees have had to transcend the limiting conceptions they have of God in order to enter the transcendent, formless, Consciousness. In my case, I learned to appreciate that the Infinite takes joy in individual expressions; I perceived the One wearing different masks and came to appreciate those unique manifestations as being Divine. It is the Divine Mother who has manifested as this entire universe—a loving, compassionate, exacting Mother who seeks to awaken us to the fact that it is She behind the mask of humanity—nay, behind all creation, if we only have the wit to lift the veil and know Her in truth and reality.

Mother's Day is a day of recognition of how Divine Mother manifests as our own mothers and has taken direct human incarnation through our own Mother Hamilton. So, happy Mother's Day to all mothers—both human and Divine.

May 19

LIFE IS EXCITING

Portrait of Yogacharya Mother Hamilton.

We must not be afraid to face life. Life is exciting! It is ter-
rifically exciting! Each of us came with a job to do for God,
no matter how humble it is. It doesn't matter because
we can make each humble job great in God. Because the
greatness is not in the job itself; it is the spirit in which it
is done for Him—the spirit of service, the spirit of total
renunciation of self, the total uplifting and giving of ourself
to the Infinite Creator.

—MOTHER HAMILTON

Mother loved life here in the world because she had surrendered all to God, and as a result, she came to see the world as God. This rare universal vision makes us aware that the building blocks of creation itself are made up of God-stuff. Electrons, protons, neutrons, and all charged particles have come from the Infinite's storehouse because something cannot come from nothing. "And God said, Let there be light: and there was light" (Genesis 1:3). So, light itself came directly from God's creative factory, as did all else. When there is only God, and God is love, then how can we do anything but love all—even as God does?

It is human nature to be attracted to that which is pleasurable and be repulsed by that which causes pain, so to appreciate that all is God, our experience must rise above the two forces of attraction and repulsion. In order to do that, we must experience a higher order of consciousness; our consciousness must rise to the level of God-consciousness in which all creation is seen as Divine. Anything less leaves us in the dual realm and entails suffering. This suffering is different than body pain; it is suffering of consciousness because we feel separated from God.

We try to arrange life so that pain is mitigated, and pleasure is maximized, but we can never remove suffering as long as we live according to the limits of the body. To know God, we must experience God. While this may seem a self-evident truth, it is amazing how many try to know God by reading books, through philosophical discussions, by doing good works, and through the reasoning mind. To experience God beyond an occasional moment of grace, we must deeply meditate, and it cannot be simply putting in time, we must actively touch the fabric of that which is God—experience His uplifting Presence, peace, bliss, and wisdom. Through this touch, we are transformed until we are a fit instrument for unbroken Divine Consciousness.

Now, we live, breathe, and act according to active Divine Will. Our life is transformed, never to be the same again. Our life is not our own in a human sense, nor do we want it to be. We exist in continuous surrender, for that is now our natural state. Victory is now ours through our surrender; the falsity of ego is but a past dream and we love life because all of life is now seen as a process of evolution toward becoming Divine. Now, our life itself is exciting because we are filled with bliss and wonder at all the works God does within and without.

A Bliss-filled Devotee

Fred Camets, an early disciple of Mother's, drove from his town just north of Portland up to Seattle every week. Fred had a humble job as the custodian of a church. His car was an older model, and it was somewhat a miracle that it made its weekly pilgrimage to Seattle with Fred at its blissful helm. Alone amongst all the disciples, Fred knelt at Mother's feet at the start of each meditation. I felt he did this for all of us—it was a custom Mother neither encouraged nor even allowed. When Fred pronamed, with his face to the floor, he was suffused with Light and Bliss. In fact, whenever I saw Fred, he was filled with an inner glow of purity. I can only imagine that the church he cleaned was blessed, because Fred was blessed.

Health Update: Recovery remains all good news for regaining the normal use of this body. From a wheelchair, I graduated to a quad walking stick with a "gait belt" around my waist that Carla holds as I walk (safety first). Then I walked into the house without Carla spotting me while using the quad cane. Now, I am walking without any cane or assistance—what freedom. I am mindful of being safe, but as strength and endurance continue to build, I continue to broaden my activities. I have walked up our driveway and up the road a ways with Carla at my side. For my left arm, I am using a small barbell weight to improve strength.

All in all, I am happy with the progress. Saw my surgeon this past week. Dr. S. said he was amazed at my progress—he really couldn't believe it. Dr. S. did have some news that was not so welcome. The results of my PET scan showed a dark spot on my spine at T-7, between the shoulder blades.[35] He ordered a biopsy. I will let you know the results when it comes back.

In receiving this news, I focus on what I can do today—so I send light and healing to the dark spot area. For today, I am fully engaged with getting this body strong and in perfect working order. As God is the Author of all of our beings and destinies, I leave it in His hands to see to it that all should unfold perfectly according to His will. I do all that I can to maintain perfect health. While knowing I am not this body, yet it is my part to be its good steward—so that I may continue to serve God and Gurus in all I do.

---

35   The Positron Emission Tomography (PET) scan uses a tracer radioactive drug to show the biochemical and metabolic state of tissues and organs.

May 26

TO FIGHT ON

Hanuman: In sacred Hindu texts, he is the
epitome of pure devotion and unconquerable will,
drawing by Gargi (Lakshmi), Anandashram, India.

We can retreat in life or fight on for progress. Each day, we are on a battlefield of some sort and each day, we decide what we are to do. For so many years, my battlefield was on the inner plane—daily meditation, working in the world without attachment to outcomes, my mind focused on God—these were my battlegrounds. Then, God directed me out of the work world and put me solidly face to face with myself, in hand-to-hand combat through deepening meditation—there is no greater discipline than this.

More recently, God has seen fit that this body should be a focus for yet another battleground. First, over three years ago, melanoma was found in the small intestines, and then in the liver: these were removed by surgery. Then two months ago, a hemorrhagic stroke the size of a lemon in my right hemisphere had the real possibility of killing this body. But, through God and Guru's Grace, extensive healthcare, intensive prayers, and a determined will, I made a dramatic recovery according to all the doctors and caregivers.

This past week, I have had a viral infection that has really taken the wind out of my sails. It is slowly improving now. Earlier this week, I went in for an MRI scan of the brain, and on Saturday, my saintly surgeon doctor called with the results. I have two spots on my brain that are "suspicious," meaning, he thinks they are spots of melanoma. If his reading of the results is confirmed, then he recommends radiation treatment. I also have a spot on my spine which will be biopsied this next Thursday. If this is also melanoma, which he suspects, then they will take tissue from the biopsy and create a concoction to inject back into the body to trigger the immune system to look for melanoma and destroy it; this is called immunotherapy.

While this is a lot of news, it is by no means all dire. We have discovered the spots on the brain before they could create more strokes; the biopsy from the spine may yield the means for a lasting treatment that keeps the melanoma at bay. While I am weaker from the virus, God has left intact my tremendous desire to fight for perfect health, and He has given me a first-class health system, and you, my first class-prayer warriors, at my side. For that, I am remarkably thankful. I could write volumes about Carla's perfect seva during all this time, and the many, many gifts of kindness from gentle and loving devotees.

What I am sorry for is not being able to spend more time with you, but the doctor has stressed, and my experience has shown me, that my brain and body continue to need rest for full recovery. So please receive my greatest prayers of love and blessings to you.

P.S. Please pray for our dear M., a sincere kriyaban these many years; keep her in your thoughts and prayers as she has had a recurrence of cancer. Om Sri Ram Jai Ram Jai Jai Ram!

June 2

BE AN ENGINE FOR SUCCESS

Yogacharya Mother Hamilton
December 25, 1904 to January 31, 1991

Lord, let my attention be
for ever fixed upon Thee.
Let me love Thee,
Let me serve Thee,
Let me worship Thee alone.
Thou art All
and All in All.

Silver Anniversary of Her Mahasamadhi

Mother Hamilton's Mahasamadhi Silver Anniversary card.

We are faced with many challenges in life. How we face those challenges determines the quality of our lives. We can be fear factories, or we can be engines for success. Once the fear factory is put into action, it tends to run on its own recycled energy, unless it is intentionally shut down. Fear generates fear; only calmness brings the fear factory to a standstill.

Faith in God: He is in charge of this universe; He has a loving, caring hand and is the mover behind all events; He turns off the fuel for fear. To breathe, to focus on the ajna, and to surrender the results to God, brings calm, stops catastrophic thinking, and halts thoughts of disaster, loss, and embarrassment. We have to take ourselves in hand and really go to work to change our thoughts if we want to see real results.

The mind is very quick and will slip into the familiar worry pathway unless governed and taught to choose a more positive mode. Let us paint a new picture of ourselves so that when we meet a challenge, we automatically access our connection to God: "Lord, what would You have me do? You are the creator of the entire universe, and You have the answers I need. You have the supply that is required. I am Your child, and You must see to it that I have all I need to succeed." Then, feel that from behind the body, there is a flow of intelligence and wisdom coming as creative, uplifting thoughts. Life-force is flowing, providing unlimited energy and health-inducing radiance. There is a pipeline of abundance flowing from unknown and delightful sources.

> Though man's ingenuity for getting himself into trouble appears to be endless, the Infinite Succor is no less resourceful.
>
> —LAHIRI MAHASAYA

We are not passive participants; we are actively attuning our thoughts, words, and actions to Divine Will. We are His instrument and feel joy at His movement through us. In fact, we are so focused on doing His moment-to-moment will that fear is now in the distant past. When we are in need, we increase our prayer-demand that He give us more, and we open wider to the idea that we are His instrument. A loving father may test his child in order that he or she learns an important lesson, but a loving parent would never abandon a child; so, our Heavenly Father, Divine Mother, may test us to hone our focus of attention to be upon God alone.

Do not waste time and energy on nervousness, which has never accomplished a good and noble act; rather, know God as the ultimate resource, comfort, and guide. The quality of our life will change in remarkable ways. There is no greater or more effective way to live our life than to be God's instrument and live with full faith and confidence in His Presence.

Health Update: An MRI examination of the brain revealed a total of five melanoma tumors in the brain. There is a plan being made to use radiation therapy. According to the Mayo Clinic:

> Radiation therapy is a type of cancer treatment that uses beams of intense energy to kill cancer cells. Radiation therapy most often uses X-rays, but protons or other types of energy also can be used.[36]

The current plan is that in the next few weeks, I will have three treatments on three consecutive days. Each treatment will last approximately 30 minutes and that should eliminate the tumors. There are more details for its preparation—side effects may include fatigue, loss of hair on the spots treated, etc. After this, I will be monitored by periodic MRIs.

A biopsy was also taken this last week from the spine, the results will be known this week; if it is more melanoma, the material will be used for an immunotherapy concoction that will be created and injected back into the body to eliminate tumors. Of course, your thoughts and prayers for perfect health are of tremendous benefit—these secret prayer warrior vibrations help to explain the amazement that doctors and nurses have had at the

---

36   Mayo Clinic, Radiation Therapy: https://www.mayoclinic.org.radiation

way I have come through all that I have. I feel strong and positive that this body should go on to perfect health. Ever in God and Gurus' loving care.

June 9

THE DANCE OF LIFE

Lord Shiva dancing in the Circle of Fiery Creation.**

In dance, there are steps forward and backward. As was said about the great dancers, Fred Astaire and Ginger Rogers, "Sure he was great, but don't forget that Ginger Rogers did everything he did . . . backwards and in high heels." So, in the dance of life, there are steps forward mixed with steps "backwards."

This has been demonstrated in the "dance" I have been engaged in with melanoma. For you, dear friends, who have remained in this striving for perfect health with me, this past week must be seen as starting with some steps back, followed by steps forward. I was busy gaining strength on all fronts when on Tuesday, a sudden weakness affected my left side. As the weakness grew over a twenty-four-hour period, I realized that I could not get into the car, even with assistance. The call was put into 911, and in minutes, the firemen and an aid car appeared at the house and whisked me off to the emergency room. This past week was spent in the hospital with tests and some new treatment; fortunately, nearby, we have a first-class hospital and staff.

A steroid medication has since shrunk the tumors in my brain that had been the cause of the weakness. I am not yet at full strength, but much improved from when I went into the hospital. Now, I have returned to Camano Island for some welcome rest from the hospital regimen of frequent tests, such as an MRI from midnight to 3 a.m. (Rest for Carla too, who, as usual, was with me 24/7 in the hospital room.) The steroid use is a temporary measure as there are increased side effects with longer use.

The next phase will be targeted radiation x-rays that bypass healthy brain cells and go after the more deeply-embedded tumors in the brain—this, I find amazing. This procedure is not without risks, which could include new bleeding, but is seen as my best option. And finally, longer-term treatment with immunotherapy that works on unbinding the tumor cells wherever they may be found in the body. Implementing these last steps was greatly sped up due to my being in the hospital: a silver lining from this newest escapade—a few steps back along with more steps forward.

So, this Wednesday through Friday will witness the radiation therapy, with a possible side-effect of weakness afterward.

You will remain in my thoughts and prayers even as I know I remain in yours. God has given us each other to go to Him together; my inmost thought and prayer are not a focus upon this body and its health, but that we should all deeply commune with our omnipotent, omnipresent, and omniscient Heavenly Father and Divine Mother. My reason for going into these details is that I know you want to be kept abreast of new developments. It is my wish that, along with me, you learn to dance the dance of life, taking steps forward or backward, with the apparent ease and grace of Fred Astaire and Ginger Rogers.

God gives us lessons to free us from the uncertainties of life in the body, and to anchor us in His supreme state of Consciousness. He untangles our attachment to this body and makes us focus on His sacred love and upliftment. So, let us join in that superior Spirit that no harm can touch, and no separation can ever reach. To be forever one in Him, merged in His bliss and comfort, no matter what dance steps are being taught by our Infinite Beloved.

June 15

GOD AS YOUR ALLY

Your ally in God: Hindu Goddess Durga Ma
comes ready for Battle and Blessings.**

What tremendous upliftment in Consciousness is ours when we keep our mind on God: this is the real secret for ultimate happiness. As I sit here, I feel the indistinct boundaries around me dissolve and expand out into an ocean of bliss and purity of Spirit—centered everywhere, circumferenced nowhere.

What a beguiling Lover God is; the world generally goes by without a second thought for the "Fulfiller of our heart's desires." Rather, we lead lives of "quiet desperation," not truly ourselves or what we are meant to be. Try to convince a worldly man or woman of the extraordinary potential they carry within. They do not have the eyes to see nor the ears to hear. Just a touch of this bliss I am feeling could change indifference into unending awe.

God chooses the moment in time to reveal Himself. He plants the mustard seed that grows into a prodigious tree of realization; there the birds of Heaven may find branches of realization to perch upon.

My heart cries out to awaken all to this Mystery of Happiness that heals the world of its woes. There is no greater realization that can be had; words seem so inadequate for the task of holding all I would like to give here—so you must receive this message in the secret of your heart and soul, and feel the wings of Spirit lift you to this abode of Bliss, in order to know what I am conveying to you.

Health Note: I have received the three-day radiation treatment this past week. This was geared toward destroying the tumors growing in my brain that are responsible for the stroke symptoms I have been experiencing. As I lay on a narrow bed with a custom rigid mask on, large square and round panels rotated around me in order to target the powerful X-rays deep into my brain. With some clicking and whirring sounds, the machine was doing its job. Forty minutes later, I emerged from the treatment. I have noticed some improvements already. I am encouraged to see this ushering this body into a new era of restoration and renewal. The brain will now work towards building healthy cells to replace tumor cells. This will likely require additional rest on my part. My plan: to grow stronger, increase stamina, and function as I did before this part of the journey began.

God takes us on many adventures in this life, each adventure with its own nuances and each for its own particular purpose. To accept it as His will gives us a tremendous advantage in life—for learning and for healing. This is due to the positive, determined, attitude God engenders in us that makes us more available for expansiveness—instead of collapsing back into ourselves and into a condensed black hole of ego-self.

No matter what role God has you playing in your life, may you sally forth in joy and happy anticipation for what the Infinite has in store for you, knowing that even if you may have some dark moments to face and roaring dragons to slay, you have the greatest Ally possible at your side—at all times and in all places.

June 19

Information, Not Definition

"You don't know my Mother!"
Mother Hamilton in Cumberland, B.C., 1975.

We are all under a barrage of information from others that can appear to be from credible sources of expertise. We can choose how we receive it: as simple information or by letting it define the reality of who we are. For instance, being involved with the health care system, I have been told many things—quite often, what I am told by one is different from what another "expert" has said before.

I remember just such a moment in Mother Hamilton's life. One night, she verged on leaving the body. The doctor told the family that he did not expect Mother to make it through the night. Mother's son, Gari, said powerfully, "You don't know my mother!"

And, indeed, it was true, Mother not only continued through the night, but for years after—the doctor had delivered information based on his experience and training; it was not a definition of who Mother was.

Sri Yukteswarji, when speaking of astrology, gave this wise counsel to Master:

> The message boldly blazoned across the heavens at the moment of birth is not meant to emphasize fate—the result of past good and evil—but to arouse man's will to escape from his universal thralldom. What he has done, he can undo. None other than himself was the instigator of the causes of whatever effects are now prevalent in his life. He can overcome any limitation because he created it by his own actions in the first place, and because he has spiritual resources, which are not subject to planetary pressure.
>
> Superstitious awe of astrology makes one an automaton, slavishly dependent on mechanical guidance. The wise man defeats his planets—which is to say, his past—by transferring his allegiance from the creation to the Creator. The more he realizes his unity with Spirit, the less he can be dominated by matter. The soul is ever-free; it is deathless because [it is] birthless. It cannot be regimented by stars.
>
> Man is a soul, and has a body. When he properly places his sense of identity, God is harmony; the devotee who attunes himself will never perform any action amiss. His activities will be correctly and naturally timed to accord with astrological law. After deep prayer and meditation, he is in touch with his divine consciousness; there is no greater power than that inward protection.[37]

---

37 *Autobiography of a Yogi* (p. 105).

Replace here astrological law with any natural or human-made law, rule, or principle with the superiority of Spirit. Let human-made limitations arouse innate spiritual dynamics; let them challenge us to raise God up in pre-eminence—a superior Creator to His creation.

I have been watching a series in which they describe the great inventions and inventors of the 21st Century. Time after time, these inventors of revolutionary ideas that we take for granted today were told that what they had thought was impossible to do. They took an idea and would not let go of it. Sometimes for years and years, they stuck with it in endless experimentation. Then, the doors opened, and the answer came—the world was improved.

We have all come with a unique spark of God that cannot be replaced by another. It may be an invention, insight into Divinity/Truth, a simple service to another, raising our family, performing at work—it may seem mundane, but that is only the limit of our vision. Sacred forces are at work in our life. The more we consciously access that fact, the greater God will reveal what we have come to express of His Light, Love, and Intelligence.

The veil of maya can lower like a curtain and make us believe there is only so much and not more. In our response, we let that limitation arouse in us unlimited Spirit. It is then that we set ourselves a new course with open-ended potential. It is true we may find that we are immediately surrounded by limitations. But each limitation can only arouse greater focus on God, Light, Love, and Intelligence. We need a determined will to propel us to seek out and consciously connect with the Creator of all that we see, and much, much more; then, we take the first steps to free ourself of the tyranny of human-made limits.

When Gari said, "You don't know my mother!" He set off a revolution and touched on the Divinity in the form of our dear Mother whose Light continues to embellish the heavens and emblazons a trail to Spirit's vast potential.

June 22

THE ROCK OF REALIZATION

Jesus Returning the Keys to Peter, painting
by Jean Auguste Dominique, 1820.

Peter's proclamation:

He saith unto them, "But whom say ye that I am?" And
Simon Peter answered and said, "Thou art the Christ, the
Son of the living God." And Jesus answered and said unto
him, "Blessed art thou, Simon Barjona: for flesh and blood
hath not revealed it unto thee, but my Father which is in
heaven." And I say also unto thee, "That thou art Peter,
and upon this rock, I will build my church; and the gates
of hell shall not prevail against it" (Matthew 16:15–18).

In this exchange between Master and disciple, Jesus immediately recognized that the Truth Peter articulated came from the power of his heavenly Father. This Truth is more than thought—more than the reasoning mind can conjure up. It is the kind of direct revelation that charges body and soul right down to the cellular level, and its clarity lifts the whole being of the devotee into higher realms.

It was with the power of this Truth that Jesus was to build his church of Self-realization. As the master gathered his disciples to himself, he was bringing constituent parts of the whole of humankind together and revealing higher Truth to them so that they would become active conduits for realized thought and service to this world—bringing Christ Consciousness to individuals first, and then to greater humankind. Jesus' work continues to this day in all sincere devotees of Truth.

Renaming Simon Barjona with "Peter," which means "the unmovable rock of realization," meant Peter was being transformed by his revelation into a higher order of disciple. The fickle human mind will question itself and vacillate, or it sets up a false pretense of knowing what it truly does not know. Only Supreme Truth revealed directly from our Father-God goes beyond duality's hold and has the power to resist the gates of hell (delusive ignorance) that will not be able to prevail against it.

To have such a revelation requires that we go beyond mere human thought. As we deeply meditate, we will move through our own thinking world and enter into a perfect calm, a realm of inner stillness—"Be still, and know that I am God." It is in this still frame of mind that great Truth may emerge from our own depths of connection with God. It will come as self-evident Truth; it may shatter our own closely-held beliefs or it may confirm what we have thought previously to be true; only now, know it as pure Truth.

When it comes from God, it will automatically be for the highest good of all, though not all may welcome what God has given. In an oceanic mind, a tremendous Truth may rise up and leave barely a ripple, but the power of that Truth will move throughout all creation. We cannot demand the appearance of such Truth, but we can ready our soul to be receptive to it.

In meditation, when we enter our inner Temple, know that we sit on holy ground and all eternity is before us. Great revelations search us out: are we receptive to the Truth that will transform us and the world in which we live into a living Christ Consciousness?

There is no greater life to live than this.

Health Update: Yesterday, I took the first step, entering the next phase of my journey to Total Recovery. I have to say, it has been quite the adventure, starting on March 19 with a large bleed in the brain caused by the growth of melanoma tumors.

Now, I have entered the fourth time of teaching this brain/body to walk again and gain strength. Allopathic treatment has recently focused on the use of steroids and radiation treatment to shrink those tumors. This has been a prelude to the next step, immunotherapy. The protocol that was suggested to me has been in place just for this past year. It was pioneered at my local hospital, which has one of the top-rated oncologists in this field who is now my doctor—God is so kind.

I am scheduled to receive a port for infusion to be done once every three weeks, for at least the next year. Immunotherapy ramps up the immune system to seek out and destroy tumors. It also can attack some of my own healthy organs/glands, such as my thyroid. There are a lot of hypotheticals here, and while "This could happen . . . and that could happen," I feel this is a clear opportunity for moving into the future and my claim for Total Recovery.

I told the doctor, "I am here to get well." He liked hearing this positive attitude and felt it definitely contributed to better results. He said, "You are a minister?" I said, "Yes, and God is a wild-card that makes all things possible." This he also readily agreed to. So, we start out on solid footing into this next stage of the journey. It is so lovely to have you journey with me—your loving support has made all the difference. Om Sri Ram Jai Ram Jai Jai Ram!

Om Ganesh: Remover of Obstacles.

June 27

CANCEL YOUR EXPECTATIONS

Yogacharya David: A yogi sitting in equanimity, Moab, Utah, 2018.**

We, all of us, have carried expectations for how life should be. However, if we really analyze it, where did these expectations come from? Now, there are expectations that can work for us, but many do not. For instance, we are optimistic and look for good things to come. For some, if something untoward occurs, it does not dampen their positive optimism. But, for others who cling tightly to their expectations, disappointment will sink their ship in a vortex of doom.

We can really take a look at what we anticipate happening and ask: "Does this propel me forward in life, or does it hold me back?" When expectations give us feet of clay, or set our feet in concrete, we must break free if we are to progress.

We can expect others to fulfill us; our work should be different and more rewarding, maybe even self-aggrandizing, life should be easier, and God-experience should come without effort. These can be secret expectations we do not give voice to, not even to ourselves; however, they work in the background of our minds and will rob us of life-energy and joy and take us out of the rhythm of life. Here is a letter to a devotee who was struggling with just such expectations:

My Dearest One,

When the world does not fulfill us, then we must turn our attention to God as our all and all. By staying focused on the world, we look to see how it falls short of our expectations and then we feel sad, lonely, and betrayed. This is a burden and an expectation the world cannot fulfill.

So, put aside the things of this world—take your grief to God and surrender it at His feet.

Oh Lord, if You will not fill my heart by those around me, then fulfill me by pouring your Self directly into my heart and soul. Be the balm of Spirit that heals my lacerated Soul. Only You can make me feel whole. You have put me on this Spiritual Journey of oneness, and only You can make my happiness complete. I cancel my expectations for this world that I have carried for so long and I give myself to You—heart, mind, and Soul.

Spiritually, free yourself from this burden. It is the material mind that thinks, "If I only had a different situation, then I would be happy." But, is it so? God is with you in infinite Joy—why not find Him here and now?

With eternal love and blessings,
DAVID

June 30

PROOF AGAINST THE OPPOSITES

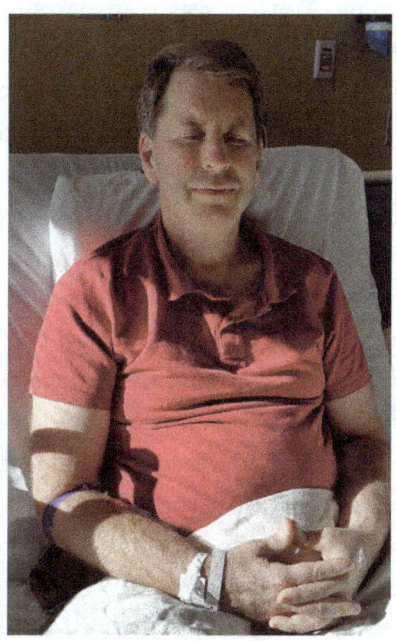

From the beginning to today, feeling God's
Presence and Bliss—Moab hospital, 2015.

From the beginning of my Spiritual Quest that God set me on, my spiritual practice was driven by necessity as well as by a spirit of scientific inquiry. Necessity was the crisis I found myself in from my late teens onward—driven by emotional/spiritual pain. The scientific spirit of inquiry was my determination to know the absolute truth about life and its ultimate meaning.

Then I met Mother. She taught from a state of realized truth that was a result of her Spiritual liberation. Far from asking me to be a blind follower based on faith, asking me to check my reason at the door, all she taught was logical, it made sense, and promised this goal: I could directly realize the same truth and experience that same level of liberation described by saints around the world. Sign me up!

From the beginning, Mother was transparent about the difficulties entailed in realizing this truth—it would not be a cakewalk. It was the "Pearl of Great Price," and it included a process of transformation she called "The Mystical Crucifixion:" we must be prepared to give all in order to receive all. If I had not been driven by an inborn necessity, my natural entropy may have eventually exhausted itself and I would have sought what would appear to be an easier life of simply living in the world, as many others satisfy themselves with. Fortunately, I say now, the inner pain would not allow me to rest in this way—now, I consider that painful crisis a result of transcendent grace.

Through many years of undergoing the Mystical Crucifixion, and the gradual transformation that resulted, I can observe the results of following this journey that God and Guru have set me on. Throughout it all, I determined to stick to only what my experience taught me, not adding layers of philosophical speculation—I was only interested in practical, realized truth.

One of the things we are taught by the world's great spiritual masters: this world is filled with opposites—for every high, there is a low, and with every pleasure comes pain—and that only by attaining transcendent God-consciousness can we know a state of being that is proof against opposites. As Swami Satchidananda stated it, "Bliss has no opposite."

I think anyone following these discourses over the last four years would agree that my life has had its challenges—some pretty big ones. Putting on my scientific inquiry hat—fact, no fluff—I have observed that what Mother and the great masters have taught is true. This quote from Mother:

If you will put your full attention upon God, He will open up whole new worlds for you. He will take you places that you never even dreamed of. He will actually help you to rise above these limitations, which are keeping you in the consciousness that you are the body. He will show you what you should do for the future so that you may become a radiant, successful being, filled with the love and the truth and the bliss and the glory of God. This is possible. I promise you it is. I know that it is.—Mother Hamilton

Throughout the challenges of these past four years, the Divine Presence has been constant and abiding. Whether I was in a sick bed recovering from sequential operations or rehabilitating from repeated states of paralysis, God's bliss has filled me to over-flowing. In addition, His spiritual abundance of love and light has overflowed and given itself to all those around me. His direction has guided me through a maze of decisions, and through radiation and multiple medical procedures, I have had a bedrock of peace—exactly when there was much that was uncertain in the world of opposites. In short, the Divine Presence has been a constant source of what is good and right, without interruption, and that has made all the difference—it has been proof against the opposites, and it has proven that what my guru taught is the absolute truth.

July 7

THE POWER OF PRAYER

Yogacharya David in uplifted prayerful meditation, Seattle, 2005.

It was predicted that the radiation treatment would have some side effects that could take some weeks to present themselves. And, in the last two days, I have experienced hair loss, extreme fatigue, and a bit of a fuzzy brain. On Sunday, just after noontime, I had a sudden and significant lifting of fatigue, along with clarity of thought—with this immediate change came the thought that this positive change came as a result of the Seattle Group sending healing prayers. I have also been the fortunate recipient of Reiki prayers from a group of four that Phyllis has put together.

The prayers and healing energy have given me strength and rapid recovery that has held until the last two days. This direct "Feeling" of the immediate effect of these prayers has been a wonderful experience and a demonstration of the power of prayer.

I know that I have been the recipient of many prayers over these past four months. And the attendant medical staff have repeatedly expressed amazement at the rapidity of my recoveries, which I give credit to for those prayers. So, here is to the power of prayer and to your efforts in this arena. May you be richly blessed for all that you have blessed me with.

July 17

A NEW DAY IN GOD AND HIS GRACE

Artwork gift for Yogacharya David
on Guru Purnima Day, 2019.

Groundhog Day[38] is a movie about a boorish individual; the story is an encapsulation of karma and reincarnation in which the lead character must repeat his day until he realizes all that his Soul has come to learn, and he earns his freedom.

---

38   *Groundhog Day.* (1993). Columbia Films. Directed by Harold Ramis.
https://m.imdb.com

My own life, from recent times, has been filled with a repetition of medical emergencies that have taken me back to the beginning of physical rehabilitation several times: relearning to walk, regaining my physical balance, strengthening my left knee, and mentally sorting through data while not getting my mind jumbled—mental and physical gymnastics. It has been a challenge of patience and digging deeper for resilience. Time and again, the attending physical therapists have commented on the strength of my will and determination to regain the full functioning of body and mind—stating that I am the "perfect patient."

Today appeared to crown these efforts with a promise for ultimate success. There has been a dramatic leap forward in the treatment of melanoma tumors—called immunotherapy. The physician's assistant, who supports my highly-rated oncologist, explained that she did not wish to make any false promises, but she has not seen one case of immunotherapy that has not limited the growth of a tumor; this is an amazing phenomenon and one that holds the promise for escaping Groundhog Day once and for all. This is no small miracle for medical science that has found melanoma tumors a vexation and an endless trial.

Your prayers and loving/healing thoughts are yielding results, fulfilling the promise that was set out by Team Total Recovery. Thank you. I can only say this has been the fulfillment of a loving Divine hand, after a long and twisting trail of ups and downs, a time coming for the end of an ordeal of seemingly endless Groundhog Days—Be it so, Ram!

This has been a test of mettle and faith, accompanied by an army of prayer warriors: a definite time of purification. A new day in God and His Grace. Thank you, my dear Friends. Words cannot express the gratitude I feel for all the love and support I have received throughout this time of trial and travail.

Yogacharya David wearing flower garland
in honor of Guru Purnima Day, July 16, 2019.

Transcending to Spirit

Editor's Note: Yogacharya David thanks his dear Friends in his concluding discourse.

Yes, it is as if somehow Yogacharya David knew he was in the time when "the lead character must repeat his day until he realizes all that his Soul had come to learn, and he earns his freedom," as noted in his concluding, July 17, discourse.

Yogacharya David reminds us:

> Even though there are moments that seem to drag on for an eternity—a lifetime is really over in just a blink of an eye . . . We cannot arrive at our Goal without discrimination—and real discrimination is a hard-won and strict taskmaster. Just the fact that you live means there is **great purpose** for you. To know your life has meaning is grace; to know your true purpose is realization.
>
> Love **really is** the greatest gift in this world—whether it is in giving or receiving—you must receive in order to give, and you must give in order to receive. Real love is both rarer—and more common—than most would think . . . Without these loving acts, this world would be a living hell. Loving acts abound about us.[39]

He presents us with this undated poem, but from our searches, it seems to be written prior to the year 2000.

---

39   The two quotes are from 2012: *Climbing the Sacred Mountain: Poems and Prayers of a Western Yogi* (pp. 319–320).

Look Upon the Mountain High

Look upon the mountain high,
Climb straight up, don't be shy.
Feel the earth on your bare feet,
Keep on going, never know defeat.
Nightly streams of water running,
Recognition of its conscious murmuring.
Move on up the mountain high,
Don't stop, don't die.
Burning sun running through your veins,
Fire purifies and causes pains.
Keep on climbing; it's vital now,
Pain and anguish are part of the Tao.
Freedom now in the sky,
Watch out! That's just a lie.
Wake up, don't be carried away,
This is not where you're supposed to stay.
Keep on climbing though it's steep,
You're almost to the peak.
The Perfect Master is now in view,
Look upon him; you know what to do.
The all-pervading sound is now a roar;
Relax, this word is the door.
Colors abound and turn into one,
Blue is all around,
Now look to the Sun.
Here it comes in bright streaks,
Like a sun coming over a peak.
Then it bursts upon you as the one,
The trip is over; you are done.
Becoming one with the Light,

You end your intense plight.
Now if it is to be, you come back to Earth,
Be careful, don't lose your mirth.
Loneliness descends as you come down;
Joy will return, you need not frown.
Spread the message far and wide,
You have seen God's side![40]

—YOGACHARYA DAVID

Yogacharya David, Maple Ridge, B.C., 2011.

---

40   *Climbing the Sacred Mountain: Poems and Prayers of a Western Yogi* (pp. 319–20).

A TRIBUTE TO YOGACHARYA DAVID

by Rebecca Harvey

Yogacharya David: A Guru for our time.

Yogacharya David's final discourse was posted just weeks before leaving his body in Mahasamadhi on August 12, 2019. It is clear from his writings throughout his last months that he remained intensively focused on God and that God within him was holding David to the highest possible view of his situation, which was one of perfect health and total recovery.

In view of how events unfolded after his last discourse, such conviction may seem surprising, especially in one who possessed the realization of truth, which Yogacharya David demonstrated. But Divine purpose often extends far beyond the scope of our vantage point at a given moment in time. The results of that powerful intention of conscious will and indomitable positivity sent forth from God through Yogacharya David in his last months on this earth may have an effect that is more far-reaching than can be evidenced by his own physical well-being.

Yogacharya David set an extraordinary example for all of us who face seemingly insurmountable challenges in any aspect of our lives—even in the face of death. He shows we can hold fast with both hands to the divine perfection that dwells eternally in all hearts, and to remain in that perfection no matter what, in every circumstance. Through love, we come to trust God absolutely beyond any question or doubt—by trusting in Him, all things become possible. We learn that surrender does not mean giving up in defeat; rather, it means giving everything to God—the good and the bad—to abandon all that you are, and all you call your own, into His hands and to leave it all there. The peace that comes from acceptance is not a passive acceptance of human limitations or bodily conditions; acceptance is actively fighting for the best possible outcome while knowing He will do according to His will what is for the highest good for all concerned.

Looking at David lying in his bed in the hospice ward, just a few days before his passing, his beloved wife Carla asked him, "What is the purpose of this?"

David whispered a clear reply, "To focus on God."

"To focus on God." These were his parting words meant for all who could receive it deeply into their hearts and lives. To focus on God was the summation toward which Yogacharya David dedicated his life, and it was what he manifested in perfection through the final moment of his expression in this world.

❋ ❋ ❋

As described in his discourses, Yogacharya David's health declined rapidly in the summer of 2019. After his original diagnosis of metastatic melanoma in 2015–2016, all CT and PET scans came back normal, including a scan on December 29, 2018. On March 19, 2019, David was rushed to Saint Joseph's Medical Center in Phoenix, Arizona, with a hemorrhagic stroke caused by a mass on the right frontal lobe of his brain. (See the discourse from March 21: *Fierce Grace*.)

At Saint Joseph's Rehabilitation Center, Yogacharya David worked very hard at multiple daily physical, occupational, and speech therapies to qualify for discharge in a surprisingly short time. Carla stayed by Yogacharya David's side 24/7, caring for everything he needed beyond what the nursing staff attended to, even sleeping on the floor in his room until a cot was found for her. Yogacharya David's brother Jerry was also present as a help and support throughout his time in rehabilitation in Phoenix and during the months that followed.

On April 24, Yogacharya David and Carla returned to their home on Camano Island, in Washington. The ordeal of traveling exhausted Yogacharya David's still-recovering brain and body. He experienced a brief setback from the progress made in rehabilitation. Walking was again difficult for a short time; a wheelchair was needed. On April 28, he said, "Today has been exhausting, although that can fluctuate throughout the day. More than anything, God has been a driving force."

During the month of May, a PET scan showed multiple melanoma tumors in his brain and also on his spine. Yogacharya David received what was considered the best possible allopathic and naturopathic treatments available for cancer at the time. In spite of the challenges with his physical condition, he continued to communicate with those who wrote to him seeking spiritual counsel, pouring forth his characteristic wisdom and good humor, unabated. Much like his guru, Mother Hamilton, before him, he spared not one ounce of himself when it came to serving those who were in need of loving compassion, even at a time when he himself was in need of care. Also, in the month of May, Yogacharya David gave spiritual talks on Sundays, which were broadcast from his home via YouTube. On June 22, devotees were invited to gather with Yogacharya David for a kirtan (sacred songs) and group meditation, celebrating the summer solstice. There, he spoke about the importance of concentrating on the feeling of God within and keeping always in God's presence. This blessed occasion would be the last service David held.

In late June, he and Carla met with doctors to discuss the protocol for immunotherapy. Instead of beginning the treatment, Yogacharya David was hospitalized twice in July due to his feeling extremely weak and having difficulty breathing. He showed improvement each time and was discharged, but again on July 23, paramedics took him to Providence Medical Center in Everett, Washington with acute respiratory failure due to pneumonia. He remained in ICU for 4 days in very serious condition. He later told of an experience that occurred during that time, saying he had been to the threshold of "crossing over," when he inwardly heard and responded to the voice of a dear friend calling him to come back.

On July 27, Yogacharya David was transferred out of ICU to the hospital's Neurology department. It was August 2 when a room was selected for him in the Providence Medical Center A-Wing for hospice care. Carla again remained in the room with Yogacharya David, constantly by his side, fully present with him night and day.

On his first day in hospice, absorbed in union with God, Christ, and Guru, Yogacharya David dictated this transcendent message that was written down by Carla and sent via email to all friends:

This is a continuation of my working on Mother's books. The Mystical Crucifixion will be the outpouring of two great cultures and traditions that Mother received during the tremendous experiences that God put her through. It is like the outpouring of the wisdom of the ages that came to Mother as fresh revelations. Come, let us sit together under the warm Arabi skies as the ancients relate their story of how man came as God and God came as man. In truth, it is all of our story. Jesus came to earth in fulfillment of a long-held prophecy, and he will come to you when a place is held, and you put your mind on fulfilling that prophetic promise that is only to be found in you.

In order to write this to you today, I have had to, like Moses of old, cross boiling red seas, barren sands, climb fiery mountains in order to speak from mountaintops and everything in the world beyond. So, do not be afraid as you set out on this journey and follow in my footsteps.

On August 7 and 8, all were invited to come to the hospital during visiting hours for a final opportunity to see David in his physical body. Those who were able to attend were given time individually to enter his room and to sit beside his bed in deep quiet inner communion. Others, as well, who were unable to be with him in person, surely felt the same inner communion established in their hearts.

On the morning of August 10, devotees were invited to return to the hospital to sit together with Yogacharya David in his room for a silent group meditation. The number of devotees was greater than the capacity of the room; many meditated in the hall outside and in an adjacent waiting room. Yogacharya David indicated to Carla that he would like to offer his pronams to those present. She helped him bring his hands together in a final gesture of divine love. The powerful blessing and upliftment in spirit were felt by all.

Finally, on the night of August 12, the message from Carla went out:

> Dear All,
> Our beloved David passed away at 10:16 p.m. tonight. He is being welcomed into the arms of our Divine Mother and Heavenly Father. His love was felt more powerfully than I can ever express.
> —Jai Guru.

At Yogacharya David's Memorial Service, when speaking of his last days, Carla observed:

> Up until the very end, he was still very present and when I would talk to him, especially in the last few days, he didn't respond to me, but then all of a sudden, I would say something, and he would either whisper something or nod his head.
> . . . He said: "God is beyond the light."
> "God touched me on the forehead."
> "JOY, JOY—why not?"
> . . . He said he saw his circle of love expanding out from the room, the community, the country, and to all this world.

Also, during Yogacharya David's Memorial Service, Carla shared:

> On August 12, all afternoon and early evening, I felt that I couldn't stay in the room; it wasn't that I was being pushed out, or that he didn't want me there; it was more

that it was just "too full," and Ruth helped me realize David was expanding more and more and into the Light of God.

Yogacharya David taught, as Mother Hamilton did, that we are—each of us—both fully human and fully divine. In the human sense, Yogacharya David suffered with, and eventually succumbed to, the effects of fourth-stage metastatic cancer. At times, he endured pain and disability while undergoing treatment, and he experienced challenges navigating the seemingly endless complexities of the medical system.

Yet, as earlier stated, by going through very human conditions of sickness as anyone may, and death of the body as everyone does, he set an example to show how to be with God in all circumstances; how to remain conscious of that divinity within, which is untouched by the limitations of brain and body.

One of the greatest miracles bestowed by God through Yogacharya David's life was the effect he had on those with whom he came in contact. For those who had the "eyes to see and ears to hear," there was clearly something special about him. Many of the medical professionals who cared for Yogacharya David commented on his ease of manner and would say that they themselves felt better when attending him.

Countless individuals have related the transformative work that Yogacharya David facilitated in their lives, in aspects both subtle and monumental. All were brought closer to the light of God within themselves through Yogacharya David's consciousness of that same light of God within himself.

To be in his presence was to experience a profound peace and awakening to that "something more," which, deep down, many of us sense must underlie the objective world. In his own way, Yogacharya David fulfilled the promise proclaimed by Jesus, "And

I, if I be lifted up from the earth, will draw all men unto Me" (John 12:32).

From a Letter to a Devotee:

> This world will always present us with reasons for feelings of loss, but the good news is there is a solution. When we surrender all to the Infinite Beloved, giving God our joys and sorrows, giving Him our all and laying it at His feet, and really letting it go, then He takes our burden and lifts it from us.
>
> When we empty ourselves of our sorrows, our loneliness, all that weighs us down, then He may fill that emptied cup with His bliss, peace, and joy. Never forget, dear One, that you are made in His likeness and image. In your essence, you are a being of Light.
>
> When you look out through these two eyes and see only darkness, it is only a veil that has been drawn down around you. Look deeper, and you will see His Light shining in and around you. I have gone through darkness, through sorrow, and feeling alone; I have felt the grief of the world, and I know that God ever stands at the ready to lift us up, if we will let Him.
>
> It is natural to feel such grief at times, but be sure not to nurture it; give it to God. Do not be identified with it, but see it passing through you, breathing it through, letting it go. When you do this, it will pass, and God will come in and comfort you—this, I know. Be at peace, dear One.[41]—Yogacharya David

---

41   From The Cross and The Lotus Journal, September 2019 (p. 10).

Beloved Yogacharya David.

In the words of Mother Hamilton, from a talk given by her in 1972:

> That is why all of the great masters down through the ages have come—that through their own realization, their own knowledge, their own example, they can teach you that you too can become as they are. To them, believe me, there is no such thing as death. Their lives are so tremendous. The things that they write across the page of life that are there eternally for all to read, for all to see—they will never die. Because these truths, which they teach in their own name and in the name of the Lord, live in the hearts of men today, hundreds and thousands of years after the passing of their physical body, and they will continue to live when all else passes away.

REFLECTIONS FOR THE SPIRITUAL
SEEKER FROM THE GURU LINEAGE

We now have reflections from Yogacharya David's guru lineage: his guru, Mother Hamilton, his param guru Paramhansa Yogananda, his param param guru, Sri Yukteswarji, from the great Lahiri Mahasaya, from Mahavatar Babaji, and from the Galilean master, Jesus the Christ.

Yogacharya Mother Hamilton

You must go within the silence of your own soul, the sanctuary of your own soul, and commune with God there. Close all of the doors of the senses and fix your attention not upon the things you want to beg Him for, but upon Him Himself. Make your request to Him be, "Father, reveal Thyself, reveal Thyself. It is You alone that I search for. It is You alone, having whom I can ask for nothing more, because You are all things, all things. Lord let my attention be forever fixed upon Thee. Let me love Thee, let me serve Thee, let me worship Thee alone. Thou art All and All in all."

And gradually, as your consciousness expands from the type of thing you have been taught in orthodox religions, you see truly that God is in every religion. He is in every form that walks the earth. He is in every atom of space because He alone is the Creator of all things. Your vision broadens, and you see God everywhere. Your heart opens to receive the great love. Your consciousness opens to receive His wisdom, His light. And your body is filled with the power of the knowledge that you and your Father are one and that no matter where you look, there He is.[42]

Paramhansa Yogananada

Desire-propelled human beings are like uncontrollable barges rushing down the floodstream of worldly life, headed over a rocky falls of crushing experiences into the oblivion of death. The boats of wisdom-guided lives steer out of the powerful current of social convention and customs and reach the shores of all-redeeming contentment in God.

This is the great truth that Jesus urged all to heed: "If you want to enter the kingdom of God, your righteousness must exceed the ordinariness of theoretical religious beliefs and living; it must transform your consciousness and whole being. Unless you follow the real way of actual God-communion in interiorized worship in deep meditation, your righteousness shall in no wise qualify you to enter the highest state of Cosmic Consciousness, the heavenly bliss from which you can never fall again.[43]

Sri Yukteswarji

"Love is God" . . . To whatever religious creed a man may belong and whatever may be his position in society, if he properly cultivates this ruling principle naturally implanted in his heart, he is sure to be on the right path to save himself from wandering in this creation of Darkness, Maya.

---

42   Mother Hamilton, June 12, 1977: *Soar to God on the Wings of Prayer.*

43   *The Second Coming of Christ* (p. 462).

When man raises himself above the idea creation of this Darkness, Maya, and passes completely out of its influence, he becomes liberated from bondage and is placed in his real Self, the Eternal Spirit.[44]

Lahiri Mahasaya

Always remember that you belong to no one, and no one belongs to you. Reflect that some day you will suddenly have to leave everything in this world—so make the acquaintanceship of God now. Prepare yourself for the coming astral journey of death by daily riding in the balloon of God-perception. Through delusion, you are perceiving yourself as a nest of troubles. Meditate unceasingly, that you may quickly behold yourself as the Infinite Essence, free from every form of misery. Cease being a prisoner of the body; using the secret key of Kriya, learn to escape into the Spirit.[45]

Mahavatar Babaji

Wake! All your earthly thirsts are about to be quenched forever . . . Arise, receive your initiation into the kingdom of God through Kriya Yoga.[46]

---

44   *The Holy Science* (p. 97, p. 46).

45   *Autobiography of a Yogi* (pp. 314–315).

46   (p. 306).

Master Jesus, the Christ

But seek ye first the kingdom of God, and his righteousness; and all these things shall be added unto you
(Matthew 6:33).

Master Jesus, the Christ

Mahavatar Babaji

Lahiri Mahasaya

Sri Yukteswarji

Paramhansa Yogananada

Yogacharya Mother Hamilton

Yogacharya David Hickenbottom

QUOTES:

TOUCHING THE AZURE SKIES OF INFINITE CONSCIOUSNESS

We now turn to "Touching the Azure Skies of Infinite Consciousness," which presents a micro-array of quotes from the time when Yogacharya David first initiated the discourses in 2013 up to the current 2019 discourse, volume six, so the reader may have a sweet taste of Yogacharya David's legacy of teachings—a soul-force sent from the infinite.

To reflect on the full scope of quotes gathered from this discourse series, please refer to *Volume One: Quotes: Resurrect the Listening Heart and Mind*, and *Volume Two: Quotes: Seeking the Sacred Code of the Universe*.

Life Is Forever and Forevermore

It is in this life that I have sought the answers to what we call death. And I have found no finality to Spirit. Touching the azure skies of the Infinite Consciousness, I come to the conclusion: life is forever, and forever more. This ends my inquiry, and I am complete.—Yogacharya David

2013–14: Living a Spiritually Rich Life

All religious ceremonies are designed, or should be, to bring you closer to God, and if it does not accomplish its goal then the ceremony has failed you. This same principle is also true for every experience in life; all experiences should bring you closer to God. So, do not be thrown by the endless variety life displays to you; each experience is a test for you to see the Divine Spirit in every aspect of His creation.

Yogacharya David, Swami Muktananda, Carla,
and Swami Chandranauda at Anandashram, 2013.

Let the name of God ring from hills and dales and in the hearts of all, by whatever Name each one chooses to sing with love and faith. Om Sri Ram Jai Ram Jai Jai Ram!

The rhythm of time marches forward with a feeling of flow between individual and universal, not so much as distinct, but like an ocean feeds into a bay and the bay feeds into the ocean and where they meet is both ocean and bay blended together. The thought enters, "This moment, this time, is perfect."

Om Sri Ram Jai Ram Jai Jai Ram! Victory to God, Victory to the Light and may Universal Love and service forever reign in the world as its motto and practice.

The Light of Christ Consciousness has redemptive power, and as souls around this world join together in this Light, the world is reborn into higher consciousness, and the promise given at the time of Jesus may be fulfilled, "Peace on earth, and goodwill toward all men."

Start now, this very instant! No matter your current feeling toward God. Even if you feel distant, angry, or peevish, it is a "come as you are party!" Bring it to God, bring exactly what you are thinking and feeling. He has big shoulders and will not mind; it is only important that you bring yourself. Open the door of your heart and invite Him in, for God is the cure for all ills. Do this, and know the greatest love you will ever have in all the three worlds.

When you stand as an observer on the banks of the river and see/ feel your grief flowing through your own heart, flowing out in front of you—let it go, then you may experience a pain and loss that is mighty, but it is endurable, and you will have peace.

To enter the room where Master dwells means to enter deeply into your yogi's cave of meditation and deep communion with God. In a world of suffering and isolation, it comes as a great amazement to find that right within your own consciousness lies a treasure trove of union with the eternal, all blissful Consciousness of God. Without the clarion call of great souls who have themselves discovered this greatest of open secrets, who would guess at this truth?

Think of yourself as separate, apart, and alone, and you are. Think of yourself as connected to the Infinite Being, surrender yourself to it, and you become one with God.

* * *

Nature is God's Cathedral . . . To get this depth, you must have a certain attunement to the subtle world that resides just behind this gross material one . . . To feel the soul of a place, or the lack of it, to be aware of the spirit that may be present, one must be focused in the present and open to this inner awareness.

* * *

Knowing if that to God, all of His angels, and the spiritual masters, there are no secrets, there is no place to hide, and everything is known, then only a fool can believe no one will know. Jesus said it most graphically when he said, That which you think you do in secret will be shouted from the rooftops!

We must be willing to humbly accept the help that God sends us, and with a clear determination, never give up striving for freedom! Even if it is with your last breath in life you continue to strive for freedom, you will carry that determination with you into your new existence.

Hot air balloon soaring over Sedona National Park, Arizona, 2014.

2015: Re-Union of Soul and Spirit

Through the Mystical Crucifixion, the serpent fully rises to the top of the tree, or the cross which represents the man or woman whose will is fully surrendered to God's will. This ascension reverses what was done by Adam and Eve in going with the downward facing serpent on the tree of life and ultimately restores man to God.

Seek always to serve God and each other by first immersing yourself in Divine communion, then let all activity be guided by that inner Source; in this way, you will help bring about the transformation of this world so it can become a haven of peace and goodness for all.

Drugs and alcohol . . . offer a pseudo comfort that weakens the body and mind, making them dependent on a chemical substance. Rather than passing the test, drug dependence seeks solace in a prison. Free yourself today and boldly walk the earth, moving from victory to victory over limiting forces by becoming a tiger of individual will, and even better, become an instrument of Divine Will.

Yogacharya David on a hike in
Palm Desert, California, 2015.

Only Light can dispel darkness, only knowledge can dislodge ignorance, and only your sincere desire for God can make you know Him. Make sure you have a love affair with the Infinite, and worship your Heavenly Father-Divine Mother with all of your heart, strength, mind, and soul and you will find the sacred Presence a loyal and constant lover that will make you qualified to be an enlightened Being.

A life unexamined is bound to repeat errors ad infinitum until there is some regard for learning from experience.

It is vital that you get a hold of the narrative of your life, the one that you tell yourself daily. If you leave it to the habits of the past, you will go in circles and arrive back where you started, or even in a worse condition. But when you conform to the highest Light within, you rise to new heights and join the greatest of realized Beings who have ever lived.

Make your life an epic in which Light triumphs over darkness, discover vast realms of Spirit within, and be a blessing to all whom you meet; now that is a story worth telling, and a life worth living! God is not absent because He is distant; rather, you do not see Him because He is so very close to who and what you really are.

Whether it is an individual, or dozens, hundreds, thousands, or millions, prayer has the capacity to bend and re-shape reality in positive ways. One person, close to God, may have a greater effect than millions, but no prayer is lost or insignificant in the eyes of the Lord. Let each one of us deepen our communion with the Infinite and therefore be a greater conduit for His blessings going out to this creation

Buddha Statue at Dhauli Peace
Temple, Bhubaneswar, India, 2013.

Attunement with God brings strength of will to act, along with faith that doors will open according to His will. This attune-ment also gives us patience, for all is ultimately in His hands . . . Anxiousness will have us flailing about uselessly, wearing ourselves out with what turns out to be destructive actions because we are not attuning ourselves to Him.

I would remind you that the breadth and depth of Christ Consciousness cannot be fully fathomed by the human mind; so there is always more for us to experience, learn, and transform as we dive deeper and soar higher in this mighty venture of knowing God.

Do not let your mind limit you to the possibilities of what you may be as you grow in Christ Consciousness. You are a child of the Infinite, and as such, you are made in His likeness and image.

Through deep meditation, awaken awareness in your cerebro-spinal system to Pranic Life-Force, the life-giving, blissful, and all-knowing Consciousness that has the capacity to lift you up into your oneness with God. Be a pioneer in this greatest of discoveries.

2016: A True New Birth

One thing about love, it constantly wants to express itself. As I have often said, love is both a noun and a verb. First, it is like the sea, a state of Being content within its expansive Self. And second, love is like a flowing river, always moving and expressing itself. In realizing God, you simultaneously and easily have both aspects of love . . . This is the great secret of love, the more you give, the more you receive. If out of fear and resentment, you do not give, then you do not receive. All healing begins with love and wisdom, and healing ends with an immersion into love and wisdom.

Humankind is capable of the highest consciousness; however, as we see signs daily it often times responds to its lowest nature. When we, as humans, put our minds upon attaining supreme God-consciousness, then the battle between lowest and highest natures ensues. Lowest nature is selfish, greedy, fearful, and it can be vicious. Highest nature is loving, kind, and full of service.

Yogacharya David and Carla at Yellowstone Falls, Wyoming, 2016.

To attune ourselves to action based on the highest nature requires that we must be mindful of our thoughts, words, and actions. We know the difference when we are acting out of our highest nature and when we are responding to the demons within. All sincere aspirants will immediately self-correct when temporarily taken over by the seductive devilish nature and will re-align with angelic purity and Light.

First, make daily contact with God within through your deepened communion with the Infinite Spirit. Then, mindfully enter into this world of activity by expressing joy, peace, and bliss; letting these qualities saturate your thoughts and words and guide your activities. All time and space are filled with sacred vibration, so live life fully, and be an instrument of Spirit at all times and in all places.

This world is rough play—universal maya. However, when souls love one another, serve one another, seek the Light within, and in one another, this world consciousness is lifted higher, changed for the better, and thereby holds the promise of transforming this world into a peaceful garden—a garden where the lion will lie down with the lamb . . . When your life comes into balance and you have congruity between Spirit, thought, word, and action, then you have a credible claim on peace.

The real solution is to realize the Divine Intention behind all the world's activities, even the bad and ugly. With this solution alone, a peace that surpasses all understanding comes into the heart and soul—a peace unshakable. Without this solution, fear and anger will corrupt the soul, making it ugly and distorted beyond the recognition of its original design by the Creator.

＊ ＊ ＊

I see the great adventure of this life as refining and purifying consciousness, to make it ready for a true New Birth.

＊ ＊ ＊

It is God-experience alone that is the true Name of God: seeing the sacred Light, hearing the soaring AUM or AMEN, feeling the uplifting currents in the spine and brain, and expanding into infinite Spirit. Like a symphony orchestra, God can be the power of a violent storm or the sweetest touch of a spring breeze upon soft petals—God-experience encompasses all experience and is far beyond ordinary perception.

Lower impulses make you feel that your mind is being drawn away from God. You know the limiting, tortured feelings that come from following these desires. Like a honey trap, you are drawn by the cloying sweet sensations inside the trap, but once you enter in, you are encaged. God-experience frees you from the trap, but you must choose God over sweet, deadly promises... True, there are powerful forces of darkness in operation at this time. Nevertheless, build a habit of giving goodness, and it will surely return to you, just as surely as the sun rises in the morning.

You may have fear concerning some experience coming your way. Fear disconnects you from God: it builds fear upon fear and will dominate your life; it makes you think of the worst scenarios, and you feel helplessly caught. The fact that you are made in the likeness and image of pure transcendent God-consciousness is completely obliterated by the fog of fear. Surrender to God means you use your powerful will to focus your mind upon God, not the images of fear. You affirm that God is at the core of your being; it is His Light, courage, strength, mirthful-joy, and love that act as angel wings to lift you above the clouds of doubt and enclosing fear.

Rainbow in Glacier National Park, Montana, 2016.

By knowing our true Self, we cast off delusion's net and free ourself from the endless cycle of gain and loss. God Himself is working through you to bless this world. There is nothing greater in
this world than to be a conscious instrument in the hands of the
Divine. You and all those sincere in their spiritual practice invisibly
unite to lift this world up for much needed harmony, peace, light,
and love.

We find in Arjuna (spiritual warrior) exactly the right attitude in
life. This world is a battlefield of competing interests, and to run
away leaves the field to those who are driven by lower desires. If
good people do not become policemen, then those posts are left
to scoundrels and the world suffers. This is true of all positions,
from the janitor to CEOs of large companies, political leaders,
and spiritual ministers. Dharma, right action, betters the world,
adharma, wrong motives, brings suffering.

While it is true that all humankind has the Christ-seed within, for most of humanity it lies in potential only. For aspiring souls that seed awakens, sending out branches to the Light, roots deep into the Soul. It is the *tree of life* that is growing right within us! New growth captures new Light, new revelations, and ever-new bliss. This is humankind's next evolutionary step; it occurs within the devoted individual, and as more individuals burst open the shell of humanness, a forest of Christ-like souls will inhabit this earth—bringing a new era of peace and fulfilling humankind's greatest potential.

2017: Gateway to the Infinite

Chronic fear gets us nowhere, and can render us inert or direct us in absolutely the wrong direction. We must be mindful to keep ourselves in the "current" of God's will. Getting caught in the wrong current could land us in staid waters of depression, or in dangerous whirlpools of swirling, endless desires, or running into downed trees of painful situations that rip us to shreds. Sometimes we must paddle hard to avoid a wayward current; other times, we are easily kept in the God-current by keeping our mind on Him. Once we find that passageway to God-awareness, it is much, much easier than being subject to the world only.

Faith in God means we keep our mind on Him, we think of His qualities of being all-powerful, all-conscious, everywhere present, all love, bliss, and joy. We know that He is above us, beside us, everywhere about us, and securely found within us. He is guiding us and the events around us that lead us into His tremendous kingdom of heaven. Our faith brings us into harmony with Him, and we realize in greater and greater measure the truth of who and what He is, and of who and what we are. Faith such as this obliterates fear and makes us do all things in full confidence that He is ever with us, and we are ever in Him.

✳   ✳   ✳

Yogacharya David meditating in the garden at
Paramhansa Yogananda's Encinitas Hermitage, 2017.

The vast majority of people are focused on the solid-material nature of this world; some see the fluid-like movement of life-energy in and around things and people, and a few have the vision to see what cannot be seen by others, the thought-trons (Master's terminology) behind all that is—a causal realm that is much larger and more profound than all other aspects of creation. We look about us and see crystalized life-energy of this world, but there is so much more that is not visible to the naked eye. The three aspects of creation can be polluted just like water . . .

The material, energetic, and idea realms can become toxic and manifest as disease and darkness of every description: an energy of darkness may form around someone depressed, the mind may become filled with wicked thoughts, or the body may suffer due to past wrong actions. We have an eternal soul—our part of God that is not born nor does it die—it cannot be burnt, drowned, nor in any way changed or corrupted. No matter the choices we make, or the bad things we may have done (against ourselves or others), this pure element of divinity resides above the physical, energetic, and idea realms.

Life, as we think of it, is the soul manifesting through the three bodies: physical, energetic, and causal. The purified body and mind are perfect instruments for the transcendent Divine Mind, and are a blessing to ourselves and to this world. Go beyond the three realms, seek out contact with the ever-pure, eternal Self—not so we can get God to do what you want, but so that we may be an expression of what God wants us to be.

Science prides itself on observing phenomena, manufacturing theories about what it sees, designing an experiment or two, and noting if the outcomes behave according to what the theory anticipates: an admirable process for physical and psychological phenomena. However, what about Spirit that originates outside material creation? Then, the only "instrument" for measuring results is found through intuition and deep inner experience whose range is beyond that of a telescope or a microscope; what then can physical science say about the results?

All humankind is equal in the sight of God; all deserve respect, dignity, and the unalienable Rights of life, liberty, and the pursuit of happiness.

Our Soul is in inseparable union with God as His likeness—this union is pure bliss, unalloyed joy, a conscious realization of our oneness with the infinite, eternal Reality. We do spiritual practice in order to re-member, and to bring back together that which is seemingly separate. The ultimate truth is that humankind is, and ever has been, an expression of God; we are made in His image. However, we have a veil of ignorance, drawn like a curtain, that makes us believe we are forever separate.

This world is on an evolutionary climb out of the Dark Ages, and yes there are challenges; however, with God in our heart, this is a new day, a bright day full of promise and glory. God is on the move, and whether the world around you reflects that or not, it is certainly true for you as you lead the way onto the path of joy, light, and abundance—Grace operating within, without, and all about. **Put your mind on God, put your mind on God, put your mind on God** and your life is changing already—feel the peace and joy of His ever-abiding Presence right in your own heart and soul. Learn what it is to live a life without fear, always aware of His ever-abiding Grace residing in your heart, mind, and soul. Be it so!

To know the truth in its totality, you must have a calm mind. By meditating deeply, you pierce the veil of separation and realize the all-pervasive Spirit—you know truth as God knows it and through the universal vision, you realize that you cannot be separate from any part of creation. To perceive truth on this level entails more than always speaking the truth—however, speaking the truth is a pre-requisite to attaining and becoming established in this higher plane of consciousness. Those who lie, and try to cover things up, and then go on to say they represent the highest truth, cannot be what they say they are.

Remember, nothing is done in secret that will not be shouted from the rooftops! Let us be our brother's and our sister's keepers and support one another, bring out the best in one another. Our time here is short, but we are accountable for what we do, so let us do right at all times and in all places; and more than that, see all others in their true essence, as beings of Divine origins, and to be respected as such.

Keeping your mind on God translates into **not** getting seduced by sex, greed, fear, power, name or fame, and the many other traps that present themselves to you as you ascend the spinal stairway. Discernment is absolutely necessary as you build a life upwards—knowing that you must have a solid foundation and well-constructed upper stories to prepare yourself to succeed in the great quest.

When we drop the body, we will then report to the supreme Creator, who is no respecter of title, money, or position—all stand equally before the all-knowing One. Only one thing will count: the quality of our inner self—built with a lifetime of what we think, say, and do—our consciousness that exudes from our innermost being. That is what lasts, and that is what counts . . . Each one of us is to be a beneficial steward of what we have been given in this life. Taking the attitude of being a servant of the Most-High, no matter the position we hold, puts us into right relationship with power.

Aarti lights at Anandashram Bhajan Hall, India, 2013.

2018: Standing on the Threshold of Eternity

Open yourself to the unlimited resources of God, feel that abundance is flowing to you through creative ideas, the right help from others, new energy infusion, and material resources—all flowing to you, through you, and out to the world from you. You are His instrument, and God delights in making you His co-creator . . . It is the power of our thought and devotion that brings God and the masters to us, that gives us an experience with them. Deepened thought and devotion act as a magnet and make them real.

There has never been a time when ultimate truth did not exist, only that it became lost to the majority . . . The angel Gabriel is sounding his trumpet, calling all to the revelatory altar of the one true living God—it reverberates across space and opens wide the way for truth. Yes, there will be *false prophets* along the way: that is inevitable. However, there will also be true God-men and God-women who will bless this earth and all humankind, who will reveal the truth and awaken other men and women across the globe, bringing this world into higher states of illumination.

When we look at the lives of great spiritual masters and saints, we see that these unstoppable personalities fight remarkable battles on the human front—persevering when the world stands against them, giving their lives in ceaseless activity, and in some instances, literally. There is no hint of becoming flaccid when it comes to standing up for truth, virtue, and God.

Having become established in eternal Life, a true master's grace can communicate itself to a sincere devotee throughout all time, and without regard for spatial distance . . . The *electricity* of this grace is ever flowing to us: in fact, it is all around us, but only if we *plug in* and have the capacity of utilizing that flow of spiritual power can it really make a difference in our lives.

Yogacharya David viewing the
Anza-Borrego Desert, Arizona, 2018.

In the spiritual field, even as in the fields of politics, business, and psychology, there are those who come along who seek to rewrite the rules of right action, either through their public teachings or their private behavior. It never turns out well. These "false prophets" become a law unto themselves, and though they begin with a promise of freedom and liberation, they, and those around them, soon become ensnared in their own ignorance.

Whatever the form of government, legal system, and opportunities for businesses are in place, there is one immutable law that will determine the greatest happiness for the most people—the law of love. Without this guiding principle, all forms of government and legal systems are simply empty shells. Love . . . is not sentimentality, but a guiding force. When you love, you will not do things that you know will bring about harm to yourself or others. When you love, you will not act out of greed, but with integrity, evoking the principle of love for one and for all. When you pass laws and regulations, you work for the highest good of all when love is your motivation.

Besides the relatively thin layer of the subconscious mind, there is the vast Superconscious Mind—not usually directly perceived by the conscious mind. When the Superconscious Mind illumines the conscious mind, it brings inspiration, intuitive flashes of truth, and a higher order of Reality that supersedes the normal waking conscious mind and the oftentimes murky depths of the subconscious mind . . . Reality in each and every moment is a crux, a crucial space in time that holds infinite possibilities. It is only a habit of mind that makes us focus on a narrow spectrum of reality that makes us think that we and our world are not touched by a transcendent beauty, power, and intelligence. By making conscious contact with infinite Reality, we can access so much more than what we ordinarily think of as self. By claiming this higher Reality as our own, we become new, whole.

When, through deepened meditation and a purified consciousness we touch the fabric of God, we open to an infinite field of possibilities. Outwardly, our life may look much the same; inwardly, we are transformed. We now know that the Lord of the universe resides in our heart, a fountain of bliss is ever playing through our spine and brain, universal love flows through our heart, and wisdom-thoughts illumine our mind—in short, we have all that our heart truly ever longed for. This makes each moment a crux in our life, because through our divine contact, all possibilities reside in us—there can be nothing ordinary or humdrum in our life ever again.

Life can challenge us to the core, and if the goal is high (and what is higher than God-realization?), then the price must be steep. To paraphrase Krishna in the Gita: "Fight the good fight with all your strength and be ever focused on God. Whether you win or lose in the outer sense is not in your control, that is up to Me (God). But, whether you win or lose, by staying focused on Me, you win the spiritual battle by being aligned with truth ever advancing in Self-realization."

"Tyranny, like hell, is not easily conquered; yet we have this consolation with us, that the harder the conflict, the more glorious the triumph" (Thomas Paine in "The American Crisis"). When you conquer hell by realizing God, the glory of triumph is not a tickertape parade or your picture in the paper, but it is the bliss that wells up from deep within; it is the Light of your eternal Being blazing, and it is the revelation of inspired wisdom from the Infinite. Anchor yourselves in this thought in times of crisis and in times of ease: God, Gurus, and all the saints and spiritual masters who have ever tread this path of realization are with us. Awareness of the fact that "I never stand alone," means that when I touch the fabric of God's Being through remembrance of Him, I touch the glory of all that He is!

Every soul has taken incarnation with a purpose—its intention for ways to live, grow, and learn. If any one of us becomes divorced from our purpose, then it induces a crisis—it may be a full-scale, life-threatening crisis, or a simmering undertow that is a drag on our energies and sense of fulfillment. Happy is the person who is in harmony with his or her soul's purpose.

Yogacharya David in meditation near
Tonto Natural Bridge, Arizona, 2014.

As happens in any hero's journey worth its salt, the hero may fail to live up to the standards of a noble path along the way. But the hero does not give up; rather, he or she recovers and keeps going—that is what makes it a hero's journey. That is our hero's journey; we recover, and we keep going, no matter what . . . It is the sure way that leads through darkened places and into the light. We are here to individually and collectively walk upon this path of the hero, to make our way to the portal of the Infinite, then to enter into that portal, and go beyond all that we have known before. In truth, our life is the greatest story ever told; so, make it a good one, make it count.

Let us feel God's grace, even now, picking us up and helping us to put one foot in front of the other. Know that even when the bridge carrying the heavy weight moans and groans, His grace is supporting us in doing His will: His strength is ours, His grace is flowing in our veins and sinews, and His wisdom is directing us...All is in His loving hands. It is one thing to give thanks for what has been given, but to give thanks for that which is to come opens the floodgates for grace to flow to you.

2019: Writing in the Book of Life

You are continually being blessed—as Master once said:
"You have God's blessings, you have Gurus' blessings,
all that is required now are your blessings!"

My Dearest One,
When the world does not fulfill us, then we must turn our attention to God as our all and all. By staying focused on the world, we look to see how it falls short of our expectations and then we feel sad, lonely, and betrayed. This is a burden and an expectation the world cannot fulfill. So, put aside the things of this world—take your grief to God and surrender it at His feet.

Oh Lord, if You will not fill my heart by those around me, then fulfill me by pouring your Self directly into my heart and soul. Be the balm of Spirit that heals my lacerated Soul. Only You can make me feel whole. You have put me on this Spiritual Journey of oneness, and only You can make my happiness complete. I cancel my expectations for this world that I have carried for so long and I give myself to You, heart, mind, and Soul.

Spiritually free yourself from this burden. It is the material mind that thinks, "If I only had a different situation, then I would be happy." But, is it so? God is with you in infinite Joy—why not find Him here and now?

With eternal love and blessings, David June 27, 2019

Conclusion

THE ROSE BLOOMS

My friends, be not afraid. Each cross is perfectly fitted to its wearer. Yours is perfect for you, even as mine has been for me. It is Love that sees you through; it is Love that makes all possible. Go boldly forward, knowing that all is in His sweet hands, shaping your soul into His likeness and image with the utmost care. For you are not different from He; He cares for you even as you love the Infinite Beloved. It is love that gives to love—and the rose blooms in the desert.[47]

Mount Temple, Alberta, Canada, painting by Dennis Brown.

OM TAT SAT AUM

---

47   *Discourses—Volume 4: 2017: Gateway to the Infinite*. An excerpt from *The Rose Blooms from the Blood Upon the Cross*.

Appendix

Editor's Note: Yogacharya David wrote this reflection on September 3, 2017. It seems fitting to share a brief historical overview of his life in his words here. For those interested, a more detailed biography in David's own words is shared in *Climbing the Sacred Mountain: Poems and Prayers of a Western Yogi.*

In the Grip of God

I am in God's Grip, and there is no other place I would rather be. From my late teens, God prodded me towards Him, and away from the world. I did not know it was He at the time; in fact, I had no faith in any concept of God I knew of then, only that I was restless, and definitely not content with what I saw in the world. That restlessness grew into a deep spiritual pain, and finally in my extremity I turned to God, and He lifted my pain; though later, it came back—the shepherd's dog nipping at me without respite.

Then began the long journey of sadhana in which I had further glimpses of God's Light and bliss—a training of the mind to stay focused on Him through the techniques my gurudev had taught me. Those creaky doors yielded, a bit at a time, opening, then closing tight, then opening again, always with the shepherd's dog driving me on when I would have rather gone back to sleep. I even resented the shepherd's dog, thinking why could I not be happy as others seemed to find happiness in this world? Thankfully, it drove me on, for what I sometimes thought of as a curse, I now see as my greatest blessing.

And many a time I fell; many a time, I made mistakes, and suffered the consequences. Unfortunately, not only did I suffer, but those around me suffered, as well. Even through the Dark Night of my Soul, through many mistakes and missteps, Grace found a way through my ignorance, my vanity, lower human desires, and my indifference. What endless patience God and Guru gave me, never giving up on me, transforming the base metal of human-ness into the gold of Spirit—God and Guru being alchemists extraordinaire.

With many missteps on my part, I never wavered in my desire for God, and gradually that transformation took shape; a new being was born, something far beyond my ability to enact. So, while I was an active participant in the process, I was increasingly very much witness to the extraordinary forces at work in me. God-experience went from very occasional glimpses, then to a most-of-the-time Reality, culminating in an every-moment state of being.

Now I live in His grip, God's power and intelligence flowing through me, and I am witness to what He does in and around me. And I am more humbled than ever before, for the witness in me is in awe of what He is about. There is no life more fully lived than when in Him; His bliss, His grace is ever at work. And what He has shown me, what I most definitely know, is that same spark of Divinity, that same seed of Grace that has grown into a tree, is in every living soul that walks the earth.

Not all will awaken to this transformed life in this lifetime, but there are those destined to live in Him, and shed His qualities to all the earth. As one or two awaken, so that quickens the lives of others. One or two awaken over there, then there, and on and on it spreads as the world is lifted into greater heights. When a significant minority transforms—not that large of a percentage, actually—it will spread all over this earth. Suddenly it will not be about money, power, and fame, but about recognizing the Light in one another and in the world itself. Even though the world may be of no great support in living a spiritual life at this present time, there is no greater opportunity to be in the vanguard of what is to come—to help lead the way through your own example. For I can tell you from my own experience, there is no greater way to live this life than to be in the grip of God.[48]

---

48   *Discourses Volume Four 2017: Gateway to the Infinite* (p.262).

References

Arnold, Edwin, Sir. (1904). *The Song Celestial; or Bhagavad Gita.* Boston: Little Brown & Co.

Harrigel, Eugen. (1999). *Zen in the Art of Archery.* New York: Vintage Books.

Self-Realization Fellowship. (1996). *Rajarsi Janakananda: A Great Western Yogi.* Los Angeles, CA.: Self-Realization Fellowship.

Kondo, Marie. (2017). *The Life-Changing Magic of Tidying Up.* New York: Ten Speed Press.

Paramhansa Yogananda. (2004/2007). *The Second Coming of Christ. Volume One.* Los Angeles, CA.: Self-Realization Fellowship.

Paramhansa Yogananda. (1995). *God Talks with Arjuna: Bhagavad Gita.* Los Angeles, CA.: Self-Realization Fellowship.

Paramhansa Yogananda. (1984). *Para-Grams by Paramhansa Yogananda.* Los Angeles, CA.: Self-Realization Fellowship.

Paramhansa Yogananda. (1946). *Autobiography of a Yogi.* New York: The Philosophical Library.

Reverend Mother Yogacharya Mildred Hamilton. (2022). *The Mystical Crucifixion.* Seattle, WA.: The Cross and The Lotus Publishing.

Sri Aurobindo. (1995). *Essays on the Gita.* Twin Lakes, WI.: Lotus Light Publishing.

Swami Sri Yukteswar. (1990). *The Holy Science.* Los Angeles, CA.: Self-Realization Fellowship.

Tagore, Rabindranath. Translation. (1915). *Songs of Kabir*. New York: Macmillan.

Hickenbottom, Yogacharya David. (2023). *Discourses Volume Four 2017: Gateway to the Infinite*. Camano Island, WA.: The Cross and The Lotus Publishing.

Yogacharya David Hickenbottom. (2022). *Silence: Entering the Cosmic Sea of Consciousness*. Seattle, WA.: The Cross and The Lotus Publishing.

Yogacharya David Hickenbottom. (2021). *Climbing the Sacred Mountain: Poems and Prayers of a Western Yogi*. Seattle, WA.: The Cross and The Lotus Publishing.

Yogacharya David Hickenbottom. (2019). *My Spiritual India*. Seattle, WA.: The Cross and The Lotus Publishing.

Film References

Groundhog Day. (1993). Columbia Films. Directed by Harold Ramus.

Ram Dass: Fierce Grace. (2013). Ram Dass/Richard Alpert. Directed by Mickey Lemie.

Tidying Up with Marie Kondo. (2019). Executive Producer: Marie Kondo, Takumi Kawahara, Gail Berman, Bianca Barnes-Williams. Netflix.

Bible References

King James Bible Online: https//www.kingjamesbibleonline.org

Website References

The Cross and The Lotus: www.crossandlotus.com

Anandashram reference: www.anandashram.org

Image Attribution

With the exception of those listed below, all images are used courtesy of the David and Carla Hickenbottom portfolio. Photos were taken by David and Carla Hickenbottom, or gifted with permission by friends, family, and devotees. Attribution for images from these sources has not been included here. Images of devotees or written submissions from devotees are all included after receiving consent for publication in this book series. Images are either paid for or for free under public domain, Creative Commons licensing, or from other sources as noted.

January 6. Paramhansa Yogananda, 1952. Picture commonly known as *The Last Smile* by Arthur Say. Commons.wikimedia. org. Public domain.

January 9. Paramhansa Yogananda, Los Angeles, 1925. Cropped from original photo of *Paramhansa Yogananda with American Indians*. Commons.wikimedia.org. Public domain.

January 13. Paramhansa Yogananda and Rajasi Janakananda, 1938. Paramhansayogananda.com. Public domain.

January 17. *Green Forest* by Ruslan Gilmanshin on Dreamstime. com. License purchased.

January 20. *Tree of Life* by Tamasin Ramsay is licensed under Creative Commons CC-BY-SA 3.0 Commons.wikimedia.org.

February 3. *Hindu God Krishan, Gita,* lithograph by Vasudeo Pandya, 1932. Commons.wikimedia.org. Public domain.

February 8. *Jesus in the Temple,* painting by Heinrich Hofmann, 1881. Commonswikimedia.org. Public domain.

February 10. *Jesus Tempted,* painting by Carl Bloch, 1850. Wikiart. org. Public domain.

February 14. Saint Valentine icon, c. 496. Commons.wikimedia. org. Public domain.

February 17. *Shiva Gives Pashupatastra to Arjuna* by Mahavir Prasad Mishra. Mahabharata: Tej Kumar Book Depot. Commons. wikimedia.org. Public domain.

March 2. *Lotus* by Muladhara on Dreamstime.com. License purchased.

March 7. Paramhansa Yogananda, 1952. Picture commonly known as "The Last Smile" by Arthur Say. Commons.wikimedia.org. Public domain.

March 9. Sri Yukteswar and Paramhansa Yogananda, Calcutta, India, 1935. Commons.wikimedia.org. Public domain.

March 14. *Lotus Flower* by Vadim Georgriev on Dreamstime.com. License purchased.

April 21. *Resurrection of Jesus Christ* by Keith Lance on iStockphoto.com. License purchased.

April 28. *Beetles Pollinate Orange Daylilies* by Olgavolodina on Dreamstime.com. License purchased.

May 5. *Krishna Tells Gita to Arjuna* by Mahavir Prasad Mishra. Mahabharata: Tej Kumar Book Depot. Commons.wikimedia.org. Public domain.

June 9. Nataraja or *Shiva as the Lord of Dance* sculpture, c. 950-1000 a.d. Courtesy of the Los Angeles County Museum of Art. Commons.wikimedia.org. Public domain.

June 15. *Indian Goddess Durga Maa* by krhm73 on Shutterstock. com. License purchased.

June 22. *Jesus Returning the Keys to St. Peter,* painting by Jean Auguste Dominique, 1820. Wikiart.com. Public domain.

Conclusion: *Mount Temple*, Alberta, Canada, by Dennis Brown. With permission.

Acknowledgments

Yogacharya David has a unique ability to share spiritual teachings and soul-enhancing reflections in a most accessible manner—he can reach us in our day-to-day ways of being as we strive to live a purposeful life. He guides us, and, even as he laughs at himself, he still seriously advocates for a wake-up process.

It is a privilege to form what we call Team-David, a dedicated team of aspirants who willingly devote time and expertise to ensuring that Yogacharya David's legacy of teachings reaches those who long for a deeper, broader, disciplined-yet-freeing approach to life's journey.

Carla Hickenbottom, David's wife and senior disciple, has been a major support throughout the preparation and publication process. Her loving oversight and her diligence as director of The Cross and The Lotus Publishing support us each step of the way.

Rebecca Harvey has been a major ongoing link to data collection and historical document searches. She seems to know just where to find more information on most everything we need. Her keen eye also provides an astute read that catches the forever-escaping grammatical challenges. Mira Lutz, our other Team-David member for the Discourses, has an excellent knowledge of grammar. It is a gift of Grace to have such a fine team working to prepare and publish Yogacharya David's series of six Discourse volumes.

Our team also includes my editor, Zia Cole, for all the Discourse volumes—our gratitude to her for her astute eye and professional expertise

Jan Westendorp of Kato Design and Photo brings her artistic and professional book-design expertise forward when working on our manuscripts. She provides us with elegant page layouts and image-refinement support, and in so many other ways, she has helped us create a beautiful series of six volumes.

Team-David feels that Yogacharya David would be delighted to know that his unique writings and teachings are available in book form for all who seek a deeper, sacred understanding of the human condition.

About the Author

Yogacharya David Hickenbottom (1954–2019) met his guru, Yogacharya Mother Hamilton, a disciple of Paramhansa Yogananda, when he was a youth of 20. Yogacharya David became a Reverend in 1984 and Mother Hamilton bestowed the Yogacharya title to David in 1989.

The great Kriya Yoga lineage of India that came through Jesus, Babaji, Lahiri Mahasaya, and Sri Yukteswar to Yogananda, and then to Mother Hamilton, provides pathways to: an appreciation of, and a faith in, the everyday sacred, an understanding of higher dimensional wisdom, an integral intuitive knowing of spiritual truths, and the vibratory realms that permeate all that is, was, and will be.

Yogacharya David says: "An inner pain brought me to the path most unwillingly, and this inner pain kept me on the path. I put my shoulder to the wheel." He faced the crux of the spiritual dilemma—how to shift from the ego-driven lower or smaller human nature to a larger and luminous existence, intuitively attuned to our deeper and broader—vast—spiritual nature, thereby discovering the Living Truth. With this intense striving for Truth and Bliss, and with his Guru's Grace, David was carried through many years of Mystical Crucifixion spiritual experiences. His year in silence (2000–2001) established an inner state of stillness that never left him—and finally led him to his full Self-realization.

Also by Yogacharya David

2013–2019 Discourse Series:

- *Discourses—Volume One: 2013–14: Living a Spiritually Rich Life*

- *Discourses—Volume Two: 2015: Re-Union of Soul and Spirit*

- *Discourses—Volume Three: 2016: A True New Birth*

- *Discourses—Volume Four: 2017: Gateway to the Infinite*

- *Discourses—Volume Five: 2018: Standing on the Threshold of Eternity*

- *Discourses—Volume Six: 2019: Writing in the Book of Life*

Hickenbottom, Yogacharya David. (2022). *Touching the Supreme Spirit*. Infinite Calendar. Camano Island, WA.: The Cross and The Lotus Publishing.

Hickenbottom, Yogacharya David. (2022). *Silence: Entering the Cosmic Sea of Consciousness*. Camano Island, WA.: The Cross and The Lotus Publishing.

Hickenbottom, Yogacharya David. (2022). *Notes to Sadhakas*. Camano Island, WA.: The Cross and The Lotus Publishing.

Hickenbottom, Yogacharya David. (2021). *Climbing the Sacred Mountain: Poems and Prayers of a Western Yogi*. Camano Island, WA.: The Cross and The Lotus Publishing.

(Continued . . .)

Hickenbottom, Yogacharya David. (2019). *My Spiritual India.* Camano Island, WA.: The Cross and The Lotus Publishing.

And more to come, including:

Volume One: Quotes: Resurrect the Listening Heart and Mind. (2024) Camano Island, WA.: The Cross and The Lotus Publishing.

Volume Two: Quotes: Seeking the Sacred Code of the Universe. (2024) Camano Island, WA.: The Cross and The Lotus Publishing.

Davidji: A Collection of Memories. (2024) Camano Island, WA.: The Cross and The Lotus Publishing.